Barren, Wild, and Worthless

Susan J. Tweit

BARREN

WILD AND
WORTHLESS

Living in the Chihuahuan Desert

University of Arizona Press   Tucson

The University of Arizona Press
© 1995 by Susan J. Tweit
First University of Arizona Press paperbound edition 2003
All rights reserved
♾ This book is printed on acid-free, archival-quality paper.
Manufactured in the United States of America

08 07 06 05 04 03   6 5 4 3 2 1

Library of Congress Cataloging-in-Publication Data
Tweit, Susan J.
Barren, wild, and worthless : living in the Chihuahuan Desert /
Susan J. Tweit.
p. cm.
Originally published: Albuquerque : University of New Mexico Press,
c1995.
Includes bibliographical references (p.).
ISBN 0-8165-2333-9 (paper : alk. paper)
1. Chihuahuan Desert—Description and travel. 2. Desert ecology—
Chihuahuan Desert. 3. Chihuahuan Desert—History. 4. Natural history—
Chihuahuan Desert. 5. Tweit, Susan J. I. Title.
F802.C52 T93 2003
917.2'1—dc21   2002190753

British Library Cataloguing-in-Publication Data
A catalogue record for this book is available from the British Library.

Contents

For my friends—Terry, Linda, Sandra, Laura, Ursula, Craig, Carrie, Pam, Karla, Dale, Denisita—and all who speak for their own landscapes in their own voices.

And for Molly, Alice Joan, Sienna, and Heather, that their children and their children's children may always have magical landscapes to love.

Acknowledgments

This would have been a very different book without the contributions of many people. I thank all who listened to my stories, answered my questions, gave me their thoughts, and lent me their stories.

Thanks first to the Chihuahuan Desert, for teaching me.

Thanks and blessings to my family: to Richard and Molly Cabe, for sharing this writer's life and enriching it with your special selves; to my parents, Bob and Joan Tweit, for the gift of teaching me how to see and the continuing gift of your friendship and advice; to my brother and sister-in-law, Bill Tweit and Lucy Winter, and my nieces, Heather, Sienna, and Alice Joan for just being who you are; and to my grandfather, Olav Tweit.

Blessings on the University of Arizona Press for seeing the value in this book. Special appreciation to editors Patti Hartmann and Nancy Arora for your careful shepherding of the book. Thanks too, to my long-time friend and former agent, Jennifer McDonald, for your continuing faith and support.

Many hugs and thanks to my friends, my community far and near: Jean Olson, Pam Porter, Denise Chávez, Katherine Durack, Donna Cooney, Judy Darnall, Elena Linthicum, Patricia Wendel, Linda Peterson, Dale Goble, Laura Arnow,

Lisa Dale Norton, Lisa Brown, Alison Hawthorne Deming, Karla Elling, Marlene Blessing, Terry Winfield Simmons, Blanche Sobottke, Mary Ross, Dale Doremus, Carol Warden, Ursula Shepherd, Sandra Lynn, Carrie Jenkins Williams, Judy Hetland Siddle, David Love, and Anne Neale Young.

To the many people who helped along the way, answering questions, checking my facts, and helping with the research, my profound thanks. Special thanks to Donnie Curtis and the other staff of the New Mexico State University libraries—your help and expertise were priceless. For "Coming to the Chihuahuan Desert," thanks to: Linda Harris, Ken White, Maggie Rivas Rodriguez, William A. Dick-Peddie, and Pat Beckett. For "Spadefoot Toads and Storm Sewers," thanks to: Gary Paul Nabhan, Joni Gutierrez, the staff of the Doña Ana County Clerk's Office, and Manso, the world's sweetest dog. For "The Disappeared Ones," thanks to: Meli Duran, Dave Kirkpatrick, Dia Fox, Carlos Sanchez III, and Denise Chávez. For "Weeds," thanks to: Ed Miranda and the Doña Ana County Sheriff's Department, Maggie Rivas Rodriguez, Carlos Corrál, Roberto Martínez, Jim Peach and his *Journal of Borderlands Studies*, and Doug Mosier. For "Sanctuary," thanks to: Alice and Raymond Cabe, Dave Richman, Katie Skaggs, Katherine Durack, Mike Mallouf, Oswaldo "Oz" Gomez, Kathy Fesser, and Carol Warden and the staff of the New Mexico office of the Nature Conservancy. For "Terminus," thanks to: Leslie Blair, Delbert Utz, Jean Pillar, Jane Calvert Love, Bill Seager, Lauro Guaderrama, Lucy Dilworth, and Sharman Apt Russell. For "Going South," special thanks to Denise Chávez and Dierdre Sklar for the pilgrimage, to Michael Murphy for research assistance, and to Janice Bowers, whose articles inspired the essay.

Finally, thanks to my foremothers in writing: Terry Tempest Williams, Sharman Apt Russell, Teresa Jordan, Pat Mora, Denise Chávez, Ann Zwinger, Linda Hogan, Joy Harjo, and Vera Norwood.

This book represents my own opinions and feelings about the Chihuahuan Desert. Any errors or omissions are, of course, my own responsibility.

*[W]e toiled across sterile plains, where no tree
offered its friendly shade, the sun glowing fiercely,
and the wind hot from the parched earth, cracking
the lips and burning the eyes. . . . As far as the eye
can reach stretches one unbroken waste, barren,
wild, and worthless.*
John Russell Bartlett, *Personal Narrative of Explorations
and Incidents in Texas, New Mexico, California, Sonora,
and Chihuahua* (1856)

*You have to get over the color green; you have to quit
associating beauty with gardens and lawns; you have
to get used to an inhuman scale.*
Wallace Stegner, "Thoughts on a Dry Land."

*The desert is no lady
She screams at the spring sky
dances with her skirts high
kicks sand, flings tumbleweeds
digs her nails into all flesh
Her unveiled lust fascinates the sun.*
Pat Mora, "Unrefined," *The Desert is No Lady*

*I*ntroduction

It is a hot Friday evening in late spring, and my husband, Richard, and I are on the loose. Fridays are our date nights—no matter what comes, we reserve Friday evenings for ourselves, leaving our teenage daughter, Molly, at home with a book and a TV dinner. Usually by the time that date hour arrives on Friday night we are so exhausted by our roles as parents and by our fulltime outside careers that we can only summon the energy for dinner at a neighborhood restaurant. But this night, we are determined to get out of town, to explore this new-to-us Chihuahuan Desert landscape. We've packed a picnic dinner and are headed out into the desert with all of the car windows rolled down. The sun is midway towards the western horizon, but it is June, and that means hot. It is 5:30 in the evening and the temperature is 102°F, down from the day's high of 110 degrees.

We drive up the hill past the University campus, its lawns greened by sprinkler irrigation, across the interstate, past the golf course, the bank, the new apartment complex, the pseudo-adobe townhouses, and finally around the end of the long earthen floodwater retention dam, and out into the open desert. The early evening sunlight glares off the shiny leaves of the creosote bush all around. Now we are driving up the *bajada*, the skirt of sediment that links steep mountain face to level valley. Its evenly sloping surface, stippled with olive-green creosote bush, ascends towards the rocky face of the Organ Mountains, about ten miles east. Between where we are and the Organs, a solitary hump-backed mountain pokes through the bajada, sparsely clothed in grass, shrubs, and cactus.

"Where are we going?" asks Richard as he slows the car for the bump where the paved road abruptly ends and the dusty, washboarded gravel surface begins. Before I can answer, a pickup truck approaches, trailing a billowing rooster tail of buff-colored dust, and we roll up the windows quickly, his left arm and my right arm cranking in unison.

"Tortugas," I reply, pushing my sunglasses back up the sweaty bridge of my nose as I point at the small mountain just ahead. Tortugas Mountain, named for its resemblance to a giant tortoise forever ascending the bajada, rises alone, midway between the valley and the Organs. The little round-backed mountain sporting the giant "A" for the New Mexico State University Aggies has intrigued us ever since we moved here last year. Public land administered by the federal Bureau of Land Management, the mountain is currently leased to New Mexico State University for research purposes. A few dish antennas sprout from its top; a small forest of them, accompanied by rows of temporary metal buildings, sprawls over the bajada on Tortugas's west side. Signs warn the public away from the antenna field—"only classified personnel allowed"—but the rest of the treeless, desert-clothed mountain is accessible to hikers, mountain bikers, four-wheelers, horseback riders, and others via a web of rough trails. Abandoned quarries pock the limestone formations on its north side. A road winds up the mountain's south side to reach the telescopes on top. Bullet-pitted trash litters its lower slopes. Still, some hold this mountain sacred. Each December, during the village of Tortugas's fiesta in honor of the *Virgen de Guadalupe*, hundreds of people trek—some on their knees, some barefoot—the three miles from the village of Tortugas to the top of its namesake mountain for a daylong ceremony. The day includes a mass, the making of *quiotes*, ceremonial walking sticks, and much socializing and eating atop the mountain. After dark, Tortugas Mountain blazes with light, outlined by dozens of *luminarias*—bonfires—lit to signal the return trek of the blessed.

"Right around the corner, past the quarry holes, a two-track road goes up the side. We can park there," I tell Richard. I point at a steep, eroded track that climbs the mountain side.

Richard slows the car and turns off of the main road. We bounce up the slope in the car just far enough to park, and then we get out. The sunlight is still fierce enough to burn my pale skin. I slather on sunscreen while Richard pulls picnic things out of the back of the car. A thread of a breeze trickles by, hinting at relief from the day's heat.

I load salads, cookies, cutlery, napkins, and cups into a basket; Richard stows bread, cheese, and my wine and his beer into a day pack. He slings a pair of binoculars over his head and shoulders the day pack; I pick up the basket, adding to its contents several field guides on desert plants and critters.

The heat makes the air around us shimmer as we wander up the slope, picking our way carefully between the creosote bushes and the broken bottles, alert for spiny cacti and startled rattlesnakes. A few yards uphill of the car, Richard finds a

3

small clump of rainbow cactus, its stems striped like fat Christmas candy sticks in faded rings of pink, red, and ivory. All at once I realize that we are standing on the edge of an abrupt change in the desert vegetation. The monotonous cover of creosote bush that clothes hundreds of thousands of square miles around town, including the bajada just below us, no longer dominates. From where we stand to where the top of the slope meets the blue sky, the whole is grassland, dressed in patches and clumps and bunches and mats of dry grass just beginning to green up in anticipation of the summer rains: black grama hugging the ground in crescent-shaped patches, clouds of bush muhly like pale gold mist, bunches of sweet tanglehead, sideoats grama sprouting its miniature-Lakota-warrior-staff-like flower stalks. Shrubs dot the slope too: low mounds of range ratany with its minuscule, silvery-hairy leaves and deep magenta, pea-like flowers, the occasional wiry creosote bush, tall clumps of yucca, and spiny, whiplike ocotillo stems reaching for the sky. But it is the luxuriant—for the desert—cover of grasses that enchants me.

I stand transfixed—heat, sweat, dust, and tiredness forgotten. "This is what the desert used to look like!" I exclaim to Richard. The grassy slope looks as beautiful to me as a Monet painting. Compared to the monotonous expanses of olive-drab creosote bush, this grassland seems as diverse and interesting as a tropical jungle, with a variety of shapes and sizes and textures of plants, the whole awash in innumerable shades of dusty green and gold, flecked with wildflowers in magenta, chrome yellow, orange, and rose-pink. My eyes water with its beauty.

On up the slope we wander, pausing to look at plants, rocks, birds, lizards. We hear the sharp whistles of a covey of

Gambel's quail. I call Richard over to see a patch of Chihuahuan Desert flax growing in among the bunches of grass. Each threadlike flax stalk holds up one tissue-paper-thin yellow disk of a flower with a brilliant orange center. A red-tailed hawk wheels away from a perch on a rock upslope. A rock wren trills its sweet song. I stop to watch a line of harvester ants trail across the dry soil, each stout ant bearing one precious seed or other edible many times its own weight. Fiery crimson blossoms tip the spiny stalks of an ocotillo. I no longer notice the heat.

We have climbed high enough that we can see off to the west around the shoulder of the mountain. We scramble around the ridge and settle on a small rock outcrop to eat. I am unpacking the food, my mind on dinner, when Richard says, "Look!" and points downslope. Just below the rock outcrop where we sit is a huge mound of cactus stems, perhaps two hundred in all, each just a foot or so tall and a half a foot around, but together forming a dense mound four feet tall and a dozen feet in circumference, like a giant, tufted pincushion. Many stalks sprout buds the size of Richard's thumb; some have opened wide, flexing out a multitude of silky pink petals into many-rayed, starlike flowers. We briefly abandon dinner to clamber down and admire the huge mound up close.

Back up at our rocky perch, we distribute food and drink and then raise our bottles in toast to the view. Below us, the steep, sparsely-vegetated side of Tortugas Mountain drops abruptly, ending at the dusty olive slope of the bajada, which spills down to meet the wide, lush, green ribbon of the valley with its crazy-quilt pattern of roads, towns, suburbs, irrigated farms, and pecan orchards. Past the valley, we can see the whole dusty expanse of West Mesa stretching away to the jagged ridge of the Florida Mountains, on the horizon nearly seventy miles distant. Here and there, small volcanic cones stud the near surface of West Mesa, some spilling frozen puddles of dark lava. The horizon slowly swallows the golden disk of the sun, and the sky is shot with colors, first brilliant yellow, then tangerine, then blood orange. I look over my shoulder. In the east, the blue sky has darkened to indigo. The downslope evening breeze blows cool enough to raise goosebumps on my bare arms. It feels good. The colors on the western horizon imperceptibly shift to pink, then old rose, then ruddy red. The band of color grows more intense as it draws closer to the horizon.

We pack the remains of our dinner and pick our way carefully downslope to the car as the light fades. On the way, we begin picking up trash: a six-pack of empty beer bottles, still in the cardboard case; handfuls of beer cans; then two plastic bags snagged in the same shrub—treasures that allow us to pick up more beer cans, and broken bottles too. We ignore the plastic shotgun shell cases; there simply are too many of them. The quantity of trash littering the side of Tortugas Mountain would normally depress me. But this night I am euphoric at the discovery of a remnant of the desert's once-magnificent grasslands—a rare piece of wildness close to home. Nothing can dent my mood. I spot a pickup-truck-sized brake shoe but it is too heavy for me. I generously let Richard carry it. We compete for who can pick up the most trash. I snag more beer bottles and cans, and an old high-top leather sneaker. Just upslope of the car, I find the prize: a whole truck bumper, badly bent but opulently chromed. I can barely haul it downhill.

As we stow our picnic remains and our cache of trash in the back of the car, the first stars wink overhead. A coyote howls from the heavy equipment graveyard across the road, and a poorwill up the arroyo begins its soft call: "poor-will . . . poor-will . . . poor-will." Even the ubiquitous creosote bush looks beautiful in the dusk.

We climb into the still-warm car, bump slowly downhill, and head back around the shoulder of Tortugas Mountain. As the orange glare of town overtakes the dark sky, we talk quietly, holding hands. We resolve to get out like this more often on our Friday evening dates.

Months of everyday busyness come and go before we make good on our resolve. Still, each morning when I look up at the round-shouldered hump of Tortugas Mountain rising in the distance beyond our backyard wall, I remember the rich texture of the grassland, the coyote's yapping howl and the rock wren's trill, the delicate flax flowers and the spiny mound of cactus, the sunset and the stars. I can still feel the magic of that desert evening. I continue to struggle to feel at home in this hot and harsh landscape. But after that evening on Tortugas Mountain, I am hooked.

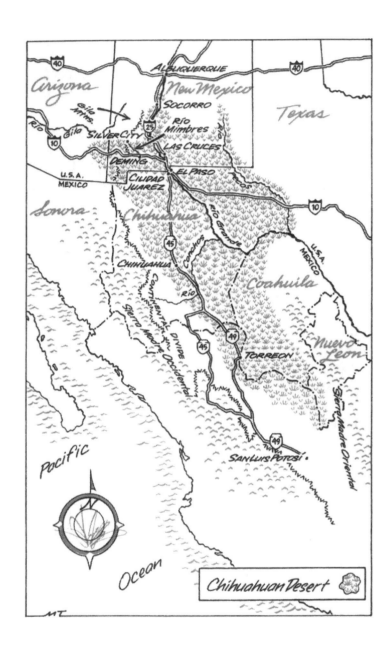

Chihuahuan Desert

Coming to the Chihuahuan Desert

It takes a long, long time to see [the desert].
It takes a long, long time to travel through it.
I asks us to redefine what is beautiful.
Terry Tempest Williams, *Writing Natural History:*
Dialogues with Authors

I live in the Chihuahuan Desert, North America's
largest desert, an unloved landscape. My house sits in the
small city of Las Cruces, forty miles north of the Mexican
border, in an irrigated oasis—the valley of the Río Grande.
Thanks to the river's water, my immediate surroundings are
lush and green, but they are misleading. Beyond this tenuous oasis lies the desert, an intensely dry landscape stretching
beyond the distant horizon, punctuated here and there by
the chiseled spines of bare mountain ranges, the whole roofed
by a china-blue sky. This is not what most people think of as
"pretty" country. Green is as rare as shade. The desert is neither soft nor appealing. Its shapes are hard and angular; the
plants are studded with spines and thorns; the animals armed
with venom and stingers. Its disquieting landscape of huge
spaces and its uncompromisingly harsh climate shrink humans and their works to a very, very small size.

The Chihuahuan Desert covers 175,000 square miles of
Mexico and the United States Southwest, an area so immense
that it is hard to picture. It is nearly three times the size of
New England or two-thirds the size of the state of Texas.
Most of the Chihuahuan Desert lies in Mexico, sprawling

between Mexico's two great mountain ranges, the Sierra Madre Occidental on the west and the Sierra Madre Oriental on the east. These two walls block moisture from either the Gulf of Mexico or the Pacific Ocean from reaching the immense area between them, hence the desert. Shaped like an elongated hand, the Chihuahuan Desert stretches north for nearly nine hundred miles, reaching into the United States. The base of the palm lies where the southern borders of the Mexican states of Durango, Zacatecas, and San Luis Potosí meet; its fingers extend across south and west Texas and into central New Mexico and southeastern Arizona. It is a long, hard drive from the Chihuahuan Desert's northernmost fingertip just north of Socorro, New Mexico, to the town of San Luis Potosí in central Mexico where the desert yields to a softer, less-harsh climate. From east to west, the desert sprawls equally far along the U.S.-Mexico borderlands, from downriver of Big Bend National Park across the seemingly endless spaces of west Texas and southern New Mexico and into southeastern Arizona.

Despite its enormous size, the Chihuahuan Desert is not well known. Nor is it a popular place. It does not inspire T-shirts, sun visors, or "I ❤" bumper stickers. Rarely do its landscapes grace calendars and coffee-table picture books. Tourists do not flock to visit this desert. Deserts are hard to love, and the Chihuahuan is especially difficult. J. R. Bartlett, surveying the Mexican–United States boundary in the 1850s, called it an unbroken waste, "barren, wild, and worthless." Public opinion still tends to support Bartlett's assessment. The Chihuahuan Desert is a landscape of almost overwhelming space—its flat basins seem to stretch beyond forever. Its sweeping expanses do not photograph well, blurred by the blue haze of distance, by searing heat, and by dust-laden winds. Its aridity is pervasive, sucking moisture equally from soil and skin, from plant and animal. Except for the intense blue of the sky, its prevailing colors are faded, as if bleached by the ever-present sun. It looks shabby. The ground between the sparse shrubs is bare as a dirt yard; windblown soil lies like dry powder on every surface. The Chihuahuan Desert seems empty, forbidding; people hurry through on their way to somewhere else.

I am no different. When I moved here, I was shocked by the starkness of this landscape, by the abject poverty associated with *La Frontera*, the U.S.–Mexican border, and by the signs that the human community, by and large, saw the desert as a dump, not a home. It looked like a painful place to live. At first, I protected myself from attachment by refusing to claim the Chihuahuan Desert as home. My home, I reminded myself, is the sagebrush country of northern Wyoming. It is an arid and spacious landscape like this one, but gentler, more immediately appealing. Less hot, less dry, less spare, it comes closer to the common definition of "beauty." Compared to the Chihuahuan Desert, Wyoming's sagebrush country is positively verdant and green. It is a matter of scale: if the sagebrush country of Wyoming is a medium oven, the Chihuahuan Desert country is the broiler. Further, the hands of humans have laid less heavily on the sagebrush country than on the Chihuahuan Desert. Loving Wyoming's sagebrush country does not hurt my heart. Too, and this is especially difficult to admit, my part of Wyoming is dominated by Anglos who look and speak like me. We share a common heritage, if not political views. Here in the Chihuahuan Desert, my pale skin and northern-European heritage mark me as a stranger. No matter how many friends I make, how many stories and traditions I learn, how much Spanish I speak, I will always be an Anglo, an other. That is uncomfortable.

Economics brought me here—literally and figuratively. My husband is a professor of economics. His salary supports our small household: Richard, his daughter Molly, now a teenager, me, and Molly's cat, Hypotenuse. Since Richard and I were married over a decade ago in Wyoming, we have bounced around like the balls in a pinball machine, searching for a place where both of us could live and work happily. We met in Wyoming; then Richard's first teaching job took us to West Virginia. That didn't last. After a year, we ricocheted west to the shores of Puget Sound in Washington State, where we both found jobs in state government. After three years of wearing suits and living on that ever-damp ocean edge, Richard missed academics; I itched for sunshine. We sold our house, packed up Molly, and headed for the drier climate and mountain edge of Colorado. In a year there, Richard finished a Ph.D. in economics begun ten years before; I wrote my first book. With newly minted doctorate in hand, Richard applied for university teaching jobs. I nurtured secret hopes that either my book would be a run-away bestseller or a job would materialize for him at home in Wyoming. Neither miracle occurred. My book sold quietly; his best offer was a two-year research appointment at Iowa State University. Having passed my childhood in northern Illinois, I moved willingly to the level landscape of central Iowa, hoping that the tallgrass-prairie-turned-corn-farms would feel like home. It hadn't in my childhood, and it didn't this time either. I missed the mountains and big skies of the West. One of the beauties of Midwestern culture is its stability, maintained in part, by an unspoken covenant to conform and to resist stretching the boundaries. I chafed at the boundaries, rubbing myself raw because I couldn't–or wouldn't—see them. I felt profoundly out of place, like a giraffe at the zoo. I was relieved when the two years ended and it was time to move again.

It was also, we thought, time to settle. The only question was: Where? Tired of compromise, of moving, I voted without hesitation for Wyoming. Molly voted for somewhere with mountains and snow. Richard, entering the highly competitive academic job market at nearly forty in a field already filled with white males like him, was the most flexible of the three of us. He simply wanted a job. We sat down with a map of the United States and after much discussion, drew a line around the area where our hopes and desires intersected with the reality of where universities are located. Our line described an elongated oval standing on end—like a balanced egg—stretching from Missoula, Montana to Las Cruces, New Mexico, enclosing much of the wide, dry spaces of the inland West. A northerner by birth and inclination, I dreaded the marginal southern edge: the deserts, landscapes that I judged too hot, too dry, too far from Wyoming's sagebrush country. As luck would have it, Richard's only job offer in the West was at New Mexico State University in Las Cruces, in the Chihuahuan Desert at the very southern tip of the oval.

No matter, I said to myself. Ever the optimist, trained like most women of my generation to compromise in order to maintain harmony in my family first and to think about my needs later, I immediately began looking for the positive side. The more that I thought about it, the more the hot desert country seemed infinitely preferable to the docile farmlands of central Iowa. The Chihuahuan Desert was, I reminded

13

myself, not really so different from Wyoming, open spaces with big skies bounded by jagged mountain ranges. Moving to Las Cruces would bring us closer to my parents now living in Tucson. Further, I had roots in the Southwest's deserts, memories of magical childhood trips combined with an inherited fascination with these difficult landscapes. My mother's grandfather, William Austin Cannon, moved to Tucson in 1903 to study the Southwest's deserts. A botanist, he focused on the adaptations that desert plants make to thrive in such harsh environments. His modest stuccoed brick bungalow, now listed as a historic landmark, still stands on the edge of the University of Arizona campus, shaded by the spreading pistachio tree that he planted. Although I never knew him—my great-grandfather died when I was just over a year old—I must carry some of him in my bones. Long before I was aware of his work, I migrated into botany in college, picking as my specialty something very similar to his main interest, the study of arid-country plant communities. (But where William Austin embraced the hot, southern deserts, I preferred the cold, northern ones.) As the leaden-gray days of late Iowa winter turned to the rainy days of Iowa spring, I convinced myself that Las Cruces and the sunny Chihuahuan Desert would make a perfectly good home.

Thus, early on a steamy June morning, I drove out of Ames, Iowa, in our unairconditioned Volkswagen camper loaded with our large tropical houseplants, on my way to Las Cruces to hunt for a house. Two long, hot days later, I crested San Augustín Pass in the Organ Mountains just east of Las Cruces. I parked the bus, climbed a nearby desert ridge, and looked west over our new home. From the rocky mountain slopes dropping away beneath my feet to the hazy western horizon, some eighty miles distant, the sere landscape shimmered in the midday heat. Except for the sky and the green swath of irrigated valley cutting across the foreground, the world that I saw was colored in a thousand shades of dry. The view was breathtaking—and sobering. Far below, the city of Las Cruces sprawled across the Río Grande valley and up the slope towards me. Beyond the valley with its city and suburbs, a level expanse of desert stretched away towards the western horizon, punctuated by the bare, dark cones of old volcanoes and by sparsely vegetated, dinosaur-spine-jagged mountain ranges. A lizard, panting in the heat, rested in the thin shade of a desert shrub near where I stood. I watched a tall dust devil skip across tan fields far below in the valley. I inhaled the dry air and squinted in the brilliant sunlight.

15

Here is a spacious landscape indeed, I said to myself cheerfully. But deeper inside a voice wailed, "It's so brown! And so hot!" I turned a deaf ear to that voice. I couldn't listen. I had to accept this Chihuahuan Desert—it was, I thought, my chance to settle in the West. It was as close to home as I was likely to get. Only now, several years later, can I admit that first horrified wail. Standing on the rocky, treeless ridge above San Augustín Pass, looking down over our new home, I did not see the promised land. My heart did not fill with love for this gritty, harsh Chihuahuan Desert landscape. I felt weary, thirsty, hot, and overwhelmed. That night, alone in my motel room, I cried myself to sleep.

The next morning I cheered up again, determinedly pushing aside any hint of disappointment. No, this is not Wyoming, I told myself, but you asked for the West, and this is the West. I set my jaw—"stubborn" could be my middle name—bent on making this place home. For me, born into a family of naturalists and educated as a botanist, that meant learning my new landscape. If I could not give the Chihuahuan Desert my heart, at least I could apply my intellect to learning about it. Some people put down roots by planting a garden or joining a church or some other social clan or starting a family; I put down roots by making the acquaintance of the landscape. As I learn to recognize and tell the stories of the birds, the plants, the insects, the animals, and the rocks, I begin to feel at home.

I once looked at landscapes only through a scientist's eyes, like my great-grandfather Cannon. Study the plants and animals, measure the climate, figure out the geology, put it all together, and you know the place. Just the facts, that's all I needed. Nor did my science include people—humans complicate the picture. My fieldwork as a professional botanist took me as far as I could get from people, to the seemingly pristine and beautiful landscapes of wilderness areas. But after a chronic disease brought me in from the field, my focus changed. Forced to slow down and stick closer to home, I now spend my days in town and nearby, where trash litters the roadsides, wild plants are "weeds," streetlights obscure the stars at night, and people's works predominate. The "field" is my backyard and the areas within the scope of a gentle walk, bicycle ride, or a short car trip; my fieldwork includes learning the stories of the landscape around me. I am no longer so arrogantly sure of what is "beautiful" or "wild." Nor do I believe any longer in a boundary between people and nature. Nature includes humans. We are part of the community of the landscape. Not only is separating humans from nature misleading; it is impossible.

After we moved here, I embarked on my own kind of fieldwork—taking a walk around my neighborhood every day, watching the world outside my windows, reading whatever I could find about this place—botany, geology, zoology, history, folk tales, literature—searching out the stories of its wild and human inhabitants. On my peregrinations, I pay close attention to the world around me, wild or not. Back at home, I write up "field notes" recording the details of my excursions. At first, it was simply an intellectual exercise. I needed to learn the Chihuahuan Desert so that I would have something to write about. I read and walked and looked and talked to experts and thought, without engaging my emotions.

The more I learned, the less comfortable I felt. I began to understand that the landscape I saw around me was a pale shade of its former self. The mind-numbing expanse of creosote bush that is now the desert had once been a life-filled grassland freckled with wildflowers, home to herds of pronghorn antelope and cities of prairie dogs. The Río Grande, now a ditch flowing between barren levees, had once wound between banks shaded by cottonwood and mesquite trees, and its free-flowing waters were home to sturgeon and turtles. The valley had once been part of the country—Mexico—whose "illegal aliens" we now attempt to keep out. The discontinuity between what had been and what is now touched my heart. The more I learned, the more painful the dissonance became. It became clear too, that I was not alone in my ignorance about the Chihuahuan Desert. Most of us who live here have little connection to this bleak landscape. The stories that would bind us to this Chihuahuan Desert come from the past, from different languages, from different cultures; they are not common knowledge.

For many people, the word *desert* conjures up a picture of a sterile, lifeless landscape, an endless reach of uninhabited sand dunes. My Webster's *New Universal Unabridged Dic-*

17

tionary defines *desert* as "an uninhabited tract of land" or "a dry, barren region, largely treeless and sandy." At first glance, the Chihuahuan Desert does indeed seem uninhabited and barren. From the altitude of a jet flying over southern New Mexico, the landscape looks like a pale corpse baked in the sun, its skin dried to hard leather, its bones bleached. There is no green carpet of plant life to soften the angular landforms. Plants grow, but only sparsely, each keeping to its own space, a decent interval of bare ground dividing it from the next. Green requires water, and water in the desert is scarce, ephemeral. Only after the infrequent rains does the earth blush with a wash of green. The remainder of the year, much of the landscape looks dead, colored only by the very structure of the earth itself—the underlying rock—a mosaic of ocher, burnt sienna, caramel, rust, tan, white, and faded olive.

Unlike the popular definition, the scientific definition of *desert* has nothing to do with barrenness. No desert is lifeless. What makes a landscape a desert is its climate, a peculiar combination of persistent scarcity and sudden, ephemeral abundance. The major characteristic of a desert climate is low and irregularly distributed annual precipitation. Not only does it not rain or snow much in the desert, the moisture that does fall is not spread evenly throughout the year. It may not rain for weeks or even months; then three inches will fall in an hour in a summer thunderstorm. Added to the undependable and scarce rain are widely fluctuating daily temperatures. From chilly night to blazing afternoon, the temperature may rise forty degrees, the climate swinging wildly from winter to summer in each twenty-four-hour period. Deserts are also characterized by extremely dry air and regular, persistent wind.

In combination, these factors add up to a climate that is

drier than it is wet, a climate so thirsty that its hot sun, parched air, and near-constant wind can evaporate many times more rain than ever falls in a year. Here in Las Cruces, our average annual rainfall is around nine inches. (As with all desert climates, the "average" embraces a wide variation: five inches per year is just as "normal" as thirteen.) The yearly evaporation potential, however, is over *thirteen times* the normal yearly rainfall, or around 120 inches! In other words, if you set a pan of water out in this part of Chihuahuan Desert, refilled it as the water evaporated, and measured how many inches evaporate over a year, the total water sucked up by the thirsty climate would equal ten feet of rain. With an environment that can evaporate more water than it delivers, it seems as if life could never survive. But life does. It adapts, in surprising and ingenious ways.

The Chihuahuan Desert really does look lifeless from a distance, especially in the searing heat of a summer afternoon. As I came to know the desert, I learned to explore by walking in the relatively cool evenings or early mornings. In these gentler times of day, the desert observed close-up reveals its magic. As the sun comes up, flocks of black-throated sparrows flit from shrub to shrub, searching for food and trailing snippets of song. Cactus wrens chatter and buzz. Woodrats forage from debris-studded middens. Hummingbirds zip from flower to flower, drinking nectar. Jackrabbits browse whatever succulent plants they can find. Grazing quail whistle softly to each other. Grasshoppers chew on the leaves of here-today-gone-next-week annual wildflowers. Small lizards sun on warm rocks, and foraging ants trail in lines across the dusty soil, sometimes marching right over the bare mounds that house the underground tunnels of kangaroo rats. As the sun heats the air, the desert quiets down, its inhabitants taking a siesta until the cool of evening returns.

Underground, the cool soil hides the tunnels, burrows, and resting places of literally millions of lives. Microscopic, single-celled bacteria flourish between the grains of soil, making their own meals from sunlight. Termites, the desert's most important recyclers of cowpies, mesquite stems, and all things woody, increase in underground metropolises. Larger animals such as scorpions, centipedes, burrowing owls, kit foxes, and snakes shelter underground too.

As dusk falls, datura and other night-blooming flowers open to release their sweet scents. The wiry stems of creosote bush broadcast a faintly medicinal odor. Owls, nighthawks, and bats emerge to forage in the air over the desert; scorpions, tarantulas, and centipedes scuttle the ground, hunting for small prey; snakes prowl for larger food; kangaroo rats and pocket mice hop about, gathering and caching seeds; sphinx moths sip nectar from flowers.

It is the plants, though, that I am drawn to. Like me, they are stuck here. The desert's plants cannot choose to be outside only in the cool mornings and evenings. Nor can they retreat to a temperate underground burrow or move away altogether when the climate deals its harshest blows. Rooted in place, they must stay and endure contradictory conditions: months of drought followed by sudden, drenching cloudbursts; summer's searing hot days and winter's freezing cold nights. During the long months when virtually no rain falls, when the soil cracks wide open and the sun bakes every surface that it touches, it seems that the plants should wither and die, their flesh reduced to weightless powder by the sun's fierce rays, leaving only their own desiccated shells. But they don't.

These desert residents not only endure—they thrive, exploding into vigorous life whenever they are blessed with the smallest amount of water. The plants are one of the Chihuahuan Desert's miracles. Every one of them has adapted its lifestyle, physical processes, and/or body type to the scarce and unpredictable availability of water. Some of them—annuals—survive the months of drought by appearing only when water is plentiful after the winter or summer rains. Like the Mexican gold poppies that some years paint the desert between Las Cruces and Lordsburg with carpets of golden yellow, these plants compress their whole lives—from birth through death—into a month or less. They germinate by the score, grow into adulthood, burst into riotous blossom, have sex, and reproduce. By the time that the soil has dried out, they are dead, vanishing as suddenly as they appeared. But they leave behind the next generation: thousands of seeds. Much of this bounty becomes food for the desert's many seed gatherers—harvester ants, black-chinned sparrows, kangaroo rats. But enough of the seeds persist until conditions are again favorable to spout and bloom, bringing their vivid colors to the desert.

21

The desert's many perennials survive the dry months with a variety of sophisticated adaptations. Cacti, for instance, store water in their own bodies to sustain themselves through long droughts. Cacti such as barrels or *bisnagas* even have pleated stems that allow them to swell after a rain—accommodating plenty of stored water—and shrink during the dry months, all without tearing the cactus's waxy skin. Further, cacti conserve their internal store of water by dispensing with leaves altogether. Like sponges, leaves transpire water continuously to the thirsty desert air. (The green, food-producing leaves once borne by cacti have evolved into spines, which help protect their juicy innards from the legions of thirsty grazers that prowl the desert.) Other desert plants, such as mesquites and acacias, have not foregone leaves. Instead, these plants do without leaves for the majority of the year but quickly sprout a flush of new green whenever water is relatively plentiful and when they can afford to lose it through their leaky leaves. Like cacti, these plants produce much of their food from their green, chlorophyll-containing stems. (Using the stems instead of the leaves to produce food is a trade-off. Photosynthesis in stems isn't quite as efficient as in leaves because the stems aren't oriented to catch the maximum amount of sunlight. But sunlight is abundant in the desert and water isn't. So the water savings more than outweigh less-efficient food production.) Some perennial plants, like creosote bush or *hediondilla*, defy logic and retain their leaves all year. In order to keep the leaves from losing so much water that they suck the plant dry, creosote bush and the other evergreens coat their leaves with a complicated layer of waxes or a fur of climate-ameliorating hairs. Such coatings help prevent sunburn too, a problem for plants as for people.

Chihuahuan Desert plants fool you. One of my favorites, ocotillo, looks for much of the year like a bunch of whiplike bare stems studded with stout spines. But when the rains come, ocotillo transforms itself. Within twelve hours after sufficient rain, tiny leaf buds dot the stems; after twenty-four hours, they are covered with a fuzz of new, tender green leaves. While the soil is moist, ocotillo lives wantonly, spending precious water, producing food, growing new cells, and blooming at a frenzied pace. As soon as the soil dries out, ocotillo drops its leaves and rests until the next rain. It seems logical that desert plants would be water misers, but that isn't always true. Many go absolutely wild after the infrequent rains, squandering water as long as their roots can pull it from the soil. But when the soil dries out, these lavish spenders do what we humans can't seem to learn to do: live without until the next rain.

The master of deception of all the desert plants is a sprawling cactus that flourishes in the bleakest parts of the desert. Hard to find, this cactus grows slender, deeply ribbed stems within shrubs or small trees such as creosote bush and mesquite. When you do find it, it doesn't look like much, just a collection of spindly, dead sticks studded with spines. Yet this cactus boasts a beautiful name, *reina-de-la-noche*, queen of the night.

In spring, buds form on the cactus's unprepossessing, several-foot-long stems, and swell, and swell, and swell. One night in late May or June, they burst open into enormous, waxy white flowers up to six inches wide and shaped like many-petaled stars. (Hence another name, night-blooming cereus, commemorating the night-opening, starlike flowers.) Each blossom broadcasts an intensely sweet fragrance on the night air, a scent that lingers vividly in my memory although I cannot find the words to describe it. The perfume is a necessary advertisement for the night-blooming flowers. Pollinators such as moths and sometimes bats follow the irresistible scent trail to drink the nectar buried deep in the flower's base. In so doing, these night-time visitors brush against the flower's sex organs. Emerging coated with a dusting of lemon-yellow pollen grains, they fly on to the next flower, delivering their load of pollen to its receptive pistil as they slurp its sweet nectar.

Reina-de-la-noche's extravagant blossoms each last only one night, and then wilt. Their ephemeral beauty is legendary. That such beauty should suddenly spring from a scrawny, ugly plant seems impossible, something born of magic. Actually, the plant saves up for its spring burst, slowly accumulating food and water in a swollen root several feet long, weighing up to thirty pounds, and resembling the parsnip from hell. This underground store fuels production of the glorious blossoms.

Reina-de-la-noche exemplifies for me the magic of this Chihuahuan Desert, a harsh, seemingly ugly and lifeless exterior capable of suddenly producing extravagant beauty.

Because it stretches over such a huge area, the Chihuahuan Desert is not the same throughout. From San Luis Potosí, near Mexico's tropical highlands, to the northerly reaches where I live, the Chihuahuan Desert slowly grades from a desert dominated by tall, multistemmed cacti, yucca (relatives of lilies that look something like many-trunked, dwarf palm trees), and other shrubs, to a dry grassland. Despite this south-to-north variation, certain plants are constant—indicators of the Chihuahuan Desert. Cacti are the hallmarks of some deserts, but not the Chihuahuan. This is a landscape identified by its shrubs, creosote bush, and tarbush, which smell like their names, thorny mesquites and acacias, gray-green mounds of saltbush, agaves or century plants with their clumps of succulent, spine-tipped leaves, and yuccas bearing tall flower stalks.

The Chihuahuan Desert where I live in southern New Mexico, now a monotonous overstory of regularly-spaced shrubs underlain by a pavementlike surface of hard, bare soil, has not always looked this desertlike. It was once a grassland freckled with a scattering of those characteristic shrubs. Until a hundred years ago, this portion of the Chihuahuan Desert sprouted grasses described by travelers as "belly high to a horse." Area residents interviewed in the 1940s remembered baling native grass hay in the late 1800s where now only creosote bush grows. Livestock overgrazing beginning after the Civil War removed the grass; subsequent soil erosion favored the deeply rooted shrubs. Groundwater pumping has aggravated the problem in some places, dropping water tables once near the surface to depths over one hundred feet. In some places, however, where the desert has been protected from overgrazing and groundwater pumping, the grassland is ever so slowly returning.

I live in the Mesilla Valley, an oasis in the desert. This north-south-trending swath of green measures sixty miles long by as much as five miles wide and is watered by the erratic flows of the Río Grande. To the north, the Mesilla Valley begins where the river passes through a narrow gap between the Robledo Mountains and a high mesa capped by a thick, dark lava flow. Past where these obstacles pinch it into a narrow channel, the Río Grande has meandered back and forth across softer sediments over the millenia, carving the wide, flat Mesilla Valley.

The head of the valley is marked by two small but rugged mountain ranges, the Robledos, their layered shales, limestones, and sandstones tilting up towards the north, and the Doña Anas, five raggedly conical peaks of reddish volcanic rock grouped in a rough circle. The Doña Anas, named for a mysterious Spanish noblewoman for whom the county and a town are also named but of whom only legends remain, are the remains of a huge volcanic caldera that destroyed itself in a cataclysmic explosion some thirty million years ago. Sixty miles south of the bare peaks of "Lady Ann's" mountains, the Río Grande kinks abruptly southeast and cuts through another narrow gap, this one called El Paso (the Pass), between the Franklin and Juárez Mountains. The foot of the valley, unlike its wild desert beginnings, is awash in the crowded sprawl of the twin cities of El Paso, Texas and Juárez, Mexico. From desert to border metropolis, this valley comprises my everyday world.

Although long from north to south, the Mesilla Valley is narrow from east to west, delineated by landforms visible from nearly every spot in the valley. The western edge is marked by an unusually level bluff—West Mesa—that rises about 250 feet above the valley. West Mesa is actually the edge of a broad surface that stretches west over a hundred miles to Arizona and south fifty miles into northern Chihuahua, Mexico. The dark cones of small volcanoes and the narrow spines of desert mountain ranges rise abruptly from its even surface like islands rising from a dry lake. Along the way, this mountain-punctuated plain rises so very gently that its ascent is imperceptible to all but the most attentive traveler. Driving west across this lake of desert one day, I was surprised to find a highway sign ninety miles west of the Mesilla Valley between Deming and Lordsburg, New Mexico announcing that I was crossing the Continental Divide at 5,845 feet above sea level, two thousand feet above my house. No ridge marks the parting of the waters here. The divide is an invisible line meandering across a grassy plain dotted with tall stalks of soaptree yucca.

Unlike the seemingly endless level surface that forms the western horizon, the eastern horizon of the Mesilla Valley is nearby and abrupt. I scan it from my backyard nearly every day, a skinny wall of dry, rocky mountain ranges running roughly north-south parallel to the valley. Off to the south are the Franklin Mountains, the shortest and most southerly section of the wall, splitting the sprawl of El Paso, and nearly touching the international border. I can see only their north end from my yard. A low, hilly gap named Fillmore Pass separates them from the next part of the wall to the north, the Organ Mountains, which, rising immediately east of Las Cruces, dominate my backyard view. The rocky crest of the Organs is the highest section of the wall. Its spirelike pinnacles, named for their resemblance to organ pipes, rise as high as five thousand feet above my backyard in the valley. A dip in the ridgeline named San Augustín Pass carries highway traffic northeast out of the valley and separates the sawtooth heights of the Organs from the undulating crest of the San Andres Mountains. The San Andres, geologically very different from the Organs, are the longest section of the wall. Shaped like an enormously long cresting wave, the San Andres stretch far beyond my horizon, disappearing from sight more than sixty miles north.

The lower slopes of the mountain wall that bounds the Mesilla Valley are buried in layers of rocky debris eroded from the peaks themselves. Ephemeral streams pouring from the rugged heights after rainstorms pick up and carry the sand, silt, gravel, and boulders chewed from the mountainsides and then abruptly drop their load where the water slows down at the edge of the mountains, forming cones of loosely packed debris at each canyon mouth. Over the millenia, the debris cones have merged to form an evenly sloping *bajada*, or skirt, of layers that smooths the transition from steep, angular mountain slopes to flat valley bottom. The bajada between the Mesilla Valley and the slope of the Organ Mountains is called East Mesa for symmetry with West Mesa across the valley. But, unlike the level edge of that western horizon, the steeply sloping surface of the bajada would make a difficult "table" indeed.

The valley itself, a green oasis in the expanse of desert, is watered by the slender, clay-colored ribbon of the Río Grande. Known as *El Río Bravo del Norte*, "The Great River of the North," in Mexico, it stretches 1,885 miles from its rise in the snowy San Juan Mountains above San Luis Valley in southern Colorado to its delta at steamy Matamoros, Mexico, and Brownsville, Texas, on the Gulf of Mexico. The Río Grande is one of only two major rivers to drain the American Southwest. Its sprawling watershed encompasses over half of that region and much of northeastern Mexico. From its birth in southern Colorado's mountains, the río runs nearly straight south through New Mexico, dividing the state in half. Forty miles downstream from where I live, the río turns abruptly southeast at El Paso. From there to the Gulf the Río Grande marks twelve hundred miles of the border between the United States and Mexico.

The Río Grande's length, enormous drainage area, and its names in Spanish and English conjure up images of a mighty river. But when I first crossed the "Great River" where it divides El Paso and Juárez, what I saw was hardly a river: Two shallow ribbons of *café-con-leche*-colored water threaded the cement-lined channel beneath the bridge. The Río Grande is a desert river, and desert rivers are inconstant. Many of the río's tributaries are dry most of the year. These desert "streams" run only during the few weeks of spring snow melt or for a

few days after summer rains. (The Mesilla Valley is at the mid-
point of a five-hundred-mile-long stretch of the Río Grande
in which not one perennial stream flows into the river from
the Jemez River in northern New Mexico to the Río Conchos,
pouring in from Mexico far downstream.) The Great River's
flow sometimes shrinks so low that it dries up on the surface
completely downstream from El Paso. It fluctuates widely
from shallow ribbons of water to occasional raging torrents.
During one such flood in 1863, the río split in two west of
Las Cruces. Before then, its channel had run between Las
Cruces and the neighboring town of Mesilla. The flood carved
a new channel on the far side of Mesilla, making Mesilla a
"malaria infested island," in the words of one disgruntled
resident, with the river on both sides. In a subsequent flood
in 1885, the whole river shifted to the far side of Mesilla,
where it now flows. In June of 1905, the Great River roared
past El Paso, carrying 25,000 cubic feet of water per second—enough water to fill an Olympic-sized swimming pool
every eight seconds! Ten years later, Elephant Butte Dam,
the largest on the río and the first big western public-works
project, built for flood control and irrigation storage, was
nearly complete. Once the dam was constructed, engineers
could begin to "rectify" the river's channel, confining the
Río Bravo del Norte to its current straightened, dredged channel between tidily bulldozed levees.

Now manipulated by engineers, dams, and earth-moving
equipment, the swelling and shrinking of its flows dependent on how much water farmers order to fill their ditches,
the great and wild river no longer lives up to either name. We
have lost more than the meaning behind its names: Gone is a
flourishing community of native fish and other aquatic lives,

29

including shovelnose sturgeon and American eel. Gone are the periodic floods spreading fertile sediments across the valley bottom land and seeding new cottonwood bosques. Gone is the unpredictability, the spirit, the wildness of a desert river.

As I learned about the Mesilla Valley, I found that it, too, had changed. When the Spanish explorer Antonio de Espejo traveled north along the Río Grande in 1582, the river was lined with "many groves of white poplar [Río Grande cottonwood]" and "thickets of grape vines and Castilian walnut trees [native Arizona walnuts]." Other reports complain of the "jungle" that filled the valley, impeding the progress of travelers and their livestock. Like over ninety percent of the Southwest's riparian—river, stream, and pond-side—woods, the lush jungles of the Mesilla Valley are no more. What was a mosaic of tall cottonwood forest, tangled mesquite *bosque* or woodland, and lush cattail and reed *cienegas* (marshes), its pattern determined by the meandering course of the river, is now a crazy quilt of farm fields, pecan orchards, towns and suburbs and, at the south end, the city of El Paso. An interstate highway runs up the east side of the valley, its twin lanes crossing the lower end of the bajada, stitching together a collection of towns, strip developments, factory-like dairies, and *colonias*—illegal subdivisions with no water, sewer, or electrical connections, home to many of the valley's poor. Stretches of creosote bush desert fill the spaces between. Old farming towns still dot the valley bottom—La Union, La Mesa, Mesilla, Doña Ana—their cores still compact clusters of adobe houses built around a central square or *plaza* and a twin-towered Catholic church, wasting little of the fertile ground. Newer development sprawls wantonly across farmland and desert alike.

At the widest part of the valley, near the north end, the interstate splits in two. One pair of concrete ribbons, Interstate 10, breaks away to cross the river and climb West Mesa, headed west through the desert for Tucson and Los Angeles. The other follows the river north to the farthest extension of the Chihuahuan Desert. Interstate 25 exits the creosote bush desert just before Albuquerque, then climbs up onto the Great Plains to head for Denver. Where the interstate highways part in the Mesilla Valley, a small city sprawls across the whole width of the valley like a spilled bowl of soup.

The city, named *Las Cruces*, The Crosses, for its location at a burial ground for travelers on the old *Camino Real*, is a recent arrival in the Mesilla Valley, laid out after the United States wrested this part of the Southwest from Mexico in the Mexican-American War between 1846 and 1848. Today, some sixty-two thousand people call Las Cruces home. With a heritage that mixes Native Americans, Spaniards, Mexicans, and Anglos (a lump term for all of us who aren't Native American or of Latino heritage), the Mesilla Valley is a diverse place. Diverse, but not necessarily diversified. Although Latinos dominate the population—just over half of valley residents are of Hispanic or *Mejicano* heritage—the names of government and business leaders, top scientists, and university administrators are still overwhelmingly Anglo.

Although divisions exist between Las Cruces's different cultural communities, economics may provide the more enduring divide. Here so close to the international border, there are more people looking for work, especially unskilled work, than there are jobs. For every one who turns up his or her nose at a $4.50 per hour job shelling pecans in a local nut-packing factory, there will be two dozen other applicants eager to earn such a princely wage. The valley is filled with hard-working people willing to work two or more jobs at barely minimum wage in order to make ends meet. This keeps salary scales low for so-called "blue-collar" and "pink-collar" jobs such as secretaries, auto mechanics, lab technicians, bank tellers, and factory workers. But salary scales for "professional" jobs—doctors, lawyers, scientists, executives, and others—must approximate those of other, wealthier places in order to attract and keep those with the option to move elsewhere. Hence, sharp divisions between the "haves" and the "have-nots." Richard's salary from college teaching and my small writing income nudge us into the "haves" range, but we have many friends who work at least as hard for much, much less. The gulf is an uncomfortable one.

Farms still carpet much of the valley, but agriculture no longer pays the bills in most households. With Fort Bliss, a sprawling U.S. Army base east of the Franklin Mountains, White Sands Missile Range across the Organs, Holloman Air Force Base next to White Sands, and the Johnson Space Center at the base of San Augustín Pass, Las Cruces has grown fat on an abundance of defense- and space-related jobs, a precarious economic base indeed in these post–Cold War times. With no industry to speak of, the largest private factory is a plant where pantyhose are inspected and stuffed into egg-shaped packages. The largest employer in town is New Mexico State University, where Richard teaches economics.

Despite our shaky, defense-spending-based economy, the housing market in Las Cruces is booming—largely due to retirees moving in. Like the rest of the Southwest, Las Cruces boasts mild winters, a relatively low cost of living, and green golf courses. But compared to cities such as Tucson, Phoenix, or Las Vegas, house prices are positively cheap. Too, Las Cruces offers a small-town atmosphere with the cultural amenities of a university town—a symphony, plays, museums, art galleries. A third of all homes sold in Las Cruces in 1992 were bought by retirees, many of them from California. (A house worth $250,000 in southern California can be bought for around half that much in Las Cruces. And for a few dollars a week, you can hire a "maid" and "yard boy" to maintain your comfortable lifestyle.) The relatively affluent retirees make a stark contrast to the other fast-growing sector of the population, impoverished economic immigrants from south of the border. Retirees and Mejicanos are not the only ones swelling the population of the Mesilla Valley. El Pasoans are moving north, fleeing the problems brought by the two-million-plus residents of the El Paso–Juárez metropolitan area: smog, poverty, and high crime rates. Although 135,000 residents may seem small compared to metropolitan areas elsewhere, the Mesilla Valley is now the second largest metropolitan area in New Mexico, and some planners predict that its population will triple by the year 2000.

33

Growth is not proceeding smoothly. Once a rural mix of farms and small towns, the fertile valley bottom is increasingly being carved up into subdivisions and ranchettes—houses with their own fiefdom of five or ten acres. Despite twenty years of community- and regional-planning regulations emphasizing preservation of the area's agricultural land for farming, flood control, and open space, exceptions to the plan seem to be the rule. On my walks and bicycle rides, I note with sadness the progression of "For Sale" signs sprouting in the fields and pecan orchards of the valley bottom. I have no particular love for the pesticide-intensive, water-wasting agriculture practiced in the valley, but the fields do provide precious open space. As each farm is carved up into private ranchettes or lots, another view of the Organs or of West Mesa disappears. The haze of orange streetlights from the sprawling urban areas now fills the valley at night, dimming the much older blaze of the stars.

Spadefoot Toads and Storm Sewers

Those toads who surprised me by coming from nowhere
after our first big rain and who sang their hallelujah chorus
on every side have surprised me again. They have disappeared as
mysteriously as they came. The desert floor and the desert air
are as toadless as ever.
Joseph Wood Krutch, *The Desert Year*

Our second year in Las Cruces was wet. I kept track of the rainfall as a cool, rainy spring succeeded a cold, drizzly winter. By the time summer's heat finally broke the spell at the end of May, we had received 7.2 inches of rain since December first, almost triple the average for those six months. Water in unusual abundance brought the desert to life. From river valley to mesa to mountain slope, the landscape was washed with a thin coat of green, as if wiped with a transparent stain. A glowing flush of tiny, new green leaves sprouted from the crooked black branches of the mesquites. The evergreen leaves of creosote bush turned from faded olive to near chartreuse. Cacti stems plumped out, filled with stored water. Yucca leaves greened up, losing their bleached look. Delicate green annual grasses sprouted from the usually bare soil along with wildflowers in every hue. Baby lizards scurried everywhere, quail raised huge broods, and the mosquitoes hatched early. The desert was flush.

One evening in May, blue-purple cumulonimbus towers built over the valley, obscuring the sky and bringing an early dusk. Thunder rumbled and gusts of cold air swept our backyard, making the long branches of the mulberry trees sway and buck like a herd of spirited horses. The thunder moved closer. Soon the storm, a real rattle-and-banger, broke. Rain pounded an insistent rhythm on the roof, stabs of lightning flashed almost continuously, and booming crashes of thunder shook our house. A bolt of lightning hit nearby with a loud "Bang!" knocking out the power. In the darkness, the drumming of the rain on the roof seemed louder, and the thunder more intense. The flashes of lightning lit up the sluicing rain like brilliant strobe lights, freezing the water for an instant in midfall. When the storm finally died down, the night was soggy. Puddles spilled over lawns and sidewalks in our suburb; water flooded the roads hubcap deep in places.

Richard and I walked into our dark backyard and listened to the storm recede. The air was cool and wet. The traffic sounds from *El Paseo*—literally "The Road"—the busy, four-lane road that runs along the east side of our subdivision, just over the six-foot-high cement block wall that encloses our backyard, were muted by the splashing and gurgling noises of running water. Lightning flickered through the storm clouds retreating uphill over the Organ Mountains; thunder boomed more softly from that distance. Shining stars in the black sky were visible through the cracks between the low, fluffy clouds overhead. A far-off chorus—not loud, but constant, insistent—insinuated itself through the splashing car traffic and the muffled thunder. I focused my attention on the sound, unraveling it from the web of urban noises that competed for my attention. It sounded like a whole flock of lost sheep bleating mournfully, accompanied by low, trilling noises as if dozens of babies shook old-fashioned wooden rattles. Richard and I recognized the distinctive chorus at the same moment. "Spadefoot toads!" we exclaimed in unison, grinning at each other with delight. The storm had summoned up the small toads from the soil to feed and call for mates. Spadefoot toads seem miraculous. Indeed, they are among the desert's most paradoxical residents. Like all amphibians, spadefoots require water to complete their life cycle successfully: They breed only while afloat in puddles and ponds, and their tadpoles die out of water. Yet these *sapitos*—little toads—thrive in the desert, where water is rare and its occurrence unpredictable. And, unlike most desert residents, spadefoots have no protection against dehydration. They possess spongelike, porous skin that, when exposed to the insatiably thirsty air, loses water constantly. With their small size—the largest species grows to 3.5 inches long and could nestle comfortably in the palm of my hand—and their leaky skin, these small toads literally mummify when exposed to the desert air, dehydrating completely in a few hours. One rainy summer evening when we left the garage door open, a spadefoot hopped into the garage sometime in the night. Closing the door the next morning, we unknowingly trapped it there. Unable to burrow in the concrete garage floor, it took shelter in the darkness between the washer and dryer. We found the mummified spadefoot there the next afternoon. To our great dismay, it had dried as hard as old leather. I picked it up and inspected it gingerly. Its eyes were gone, its once-plump skin was paper-thin and brittle, and its body was light as a discarded dove feather. I carried the sapito outside and buried it in the damp soil next to our backyard wall where it could decay and return to the earth.

Paradoxically, these water-loving amphibians prosper in the desert—not in the rare lakes and streams but in the open desert—including some of the continent's driest places. One species, Couch's spadefoot—they of the bleating sheep call—manages to thrive in the hottest, driest parts of the Mojave and Sonoran deserts where precipitation averages just 2.5 inches per year, two years can pass without a drop of rain, and summer temperatures at the ground surface may exceed a searing 160°F. How can an aquatic creature survive in such a hostile environment?

Like many desert residents, spadefoots head underground when times are too dry and temperatures too extreme. But spadefoots take the "earth sheltered" strategy to extraordinary lengths. They spend the majority of their lives—years in extreme droughts—dug deeply into the earth. Spadefoot toads can survive for as long as two years underground in solitary burrows, barely respiring, dormant. Their way of coping with the scarcity and unpredictable occurrence of water in the arid country where they live is to come to the surface only when water is abundant during the summer monsoon season. Thus, spadefoots sometimes surface for just a handful of nights each year. Their sudden appearance and equally sudden disappearance is one of the desert's summer miracles.

The little amphibians's seemingly magical ability to materialize with the rain and vanish as suddenly as they appeared has earned them the affection of desert-dwellers and has spawned spadefoot stories, poems, and songs. One of my favorites, written by folk singer John S. Thompson of Tucson, Arizona, chronicles the love affair of a raven and a spadefoot toad whom the raven discovers "singin' in the middle of the road" after a big summer thunderstorm. The two share a lovely and all-too-brief interlude before the summer rains cease, forcing the toad to bid farewell to her beloved raven and dig back into the soil again. The heart-broken raven later reflects:

You know, she's down there now, she's sleepin'
And for now, I've lost my friend.
But when a year rolls around and the rains come down
I know she'll rise again.

When they emerge, the small toads do so in torrents, like the water that they need. Their abrupt appearance is a delightful surprise—they have been absent for so long that we have nearly forgotten their existence, just as we have nearly forgotten the smell and feel of rain through the increasingly hot and dry months of spring. Then comes monsoon season and suddenly, after the first good summer thunderstorm, spadefoots are everywhere: as the thunder dies down and the rain slows, thousands of the little sapitos dig out of their solitary burrows.

On this May evening, by the time the downpour settles into a gentle rain, darkness has fallen. Richard and I splash happily off. I detour every now and then to test the depth of the puddles. Richard spots the first toad, a sapito the size of a ping-pong ball hopping down our driveway towards a puddle in the gutter. Around the curve in the street past our neighbors' dark houses we walk, treading carefully, wary of stepping on toads. Often the sidewalk and street are spotted with toads, their plump, lumpy bodies barely visible in the glow of the streetlights. At the entrance to a small culdesac, puddles spread across the road. Two pea-sized reflections shine from the surface of one puddle, a toad submerged but for its eyes. Nearby a tinier toad, no bigger than a walnut, hops down the gutter. Its back, dotted with scarlet, pinhead-sized bumps like a bad measles rash, reveals it as a red-spotted toad, the small-

39

est of our desert toads. Farther on, past the corner where we turn right onto another curving subdivision street, a huge toad, nearly twice as big as my fist, squats in the middle of the sidewalk like a toll collector. We stop to look at it, but, respectful of its wildness do not pick it up. This one is a real honker, a grandmother of its kind, five inches from rounded snout to the stub where its tadpole tail once grew. It is a Woodhouse's toad, the bullfrog of our native toad fauna.

We walk on. The rainy darkness is now quiet, the storm's violence spent. As we round the curving streets of our subdivision, testing the puddles, watching the low clouds scud by in the reflected light of the streetlights, we see more toads: toads big and small hop across lawns, squat in puddles, hunker down on the wet pavement of streets. It is these last that concern me. I wonder how many toads—nothing apparently on their minds but the business of life—die on these streets after the summer rains, caught by the bright glare of headlights and squashed flat by car wheels. The toads's sudden abundance in our neighborhood after each summer monsoon rain predates the twenty-five-year-old subdivision. The spadefoots appear here as if it was still wild desert or valleybottom bosque, not a maze of tall walls impassable to sapitos and of streets that accumulate puddles in dangerous places.

Three familiar needs drive these bug-eyed, bumpy-skinned amphibians: sex, food, and water. Water comes first. The toads that we see on our nighttime prowls are most likely headed for water—puddles, temporary ponds, rain-filled arroyos, roadside ditches—to rehydrate bodies parched by months of burial deep in the soil. After digging themselves out, emerging spadefoots hop to the nearest puddle. There they squat and absorb moisture directly through their porous skin.

(Spadefoot toads and other amphibians do not need to drink; instead they pull in water through their skin.) Once rehydrated, sapitos are ready for sex. The males float in the water and bellow their desire; the curious trills and bleats of thousands of tiny swelling throats carry for miles. Females, drawn to the din, are besieged by suitors. While she sculls in the water, he clambers atop her, holding her with special toe pads, and squirts sperm over the floating mass of eggs that she exudes. When the toads have sated their mating frenzy, they turn to the business of replenishing their stores of body fat for another long stay underground.

Spadefoot toads are not the only desert-dwellers to emerge *en masse* following the summer rains. The brief profusion of water triggers the hatching or emergence of a variety of insects, including termites, one of spadefoot toads's major foods. Several species of termites—the most common insects in the desert besides ants—stage mating flights at dusk during the summer rains. Hundreds or thousands of winged termites pour from their parent colonies, inadvertently providing a feast for the toads. But the sapitos's window of opportunity is small. The termite alates, the winged, reproductive stage, fly from their parent colony, alight, shed their wings, and mate. Only for the short time that the now-wingless termites are running about on the ground surface searching out a good location to dig a burrow, are they vulnerable to the sticky tongues of spadefoot toads. And, although thousands of termite alates may fly from one colony, each mating flight only lasts one night, and only a few flights occur each year in any one place, depending on the summer thunderstorms.

But when they occur, termite alates are a find. The toad equivalent to Dove ice cream bars, termite alates contain more

41

fat and calories than some two hundred other species of insects analyzed by scientists. The toads gorge themselves on the rich insects, eating as much as half their body weight in one night's feeding. They store so much fat that just a few nights of feasting provisions a spadefoot toad to spend a year or more dormant in its solitary underground burrow. For example, a male Couch's spadefoot—the species that must survive the longest droughts underground without food or water—can take in a year's worth of provisions in just one night, filling its capacious stomach only once, if it consumes termites. Imagine eating half of your weight in one massive feast, then becoming comatose for the next year! Or, for we females, eating two or three such stomach-glutting feasts over as many nights to nourish yourself and your potential progeny for a solitary year underground.

After a night of feeding and sex, spadefoot toads retreat into the earth. Sometime around dawn, the adults burrow into the moist soil with the digging tools for which they are named, "spades," black, hard-edged blades like ice scrapers that line the underside of each hind leg near their hind foot. They seem to swim backwards into the soil, wiggling from side to side as each powerful hind foot alternately pushes dirt outwards. The small toads dig for ten to fifteen minutes, rest for the same length of time, and then resume digging.

Spadefoot toads are not picky about their burrow sites; they bury themselves anywhere that the soil is loose enough for excavation. One warm, dry fall afternoon while digging up iris tubers from a crowded flower bed in our backyard, I inadvertently unearthed a very sluggish spadefoot toad. After checking to make sure that I hadn't injured it—it seemed fine—I sprinkled the spadefoot's skin thoroughly with water from my watering can, then quickly dug a similar hole in an undisturbed part of the garden. I carefully placed the sapito in the new hole and covered it up again, watering the dirt as I filled in the hole. The toad seemed unperturbed by the whole procedure, but it was hard to tell. I hope that despite its untimely excavation, it survived to be summoned up by the next year's monsoons.

Below ground—away from the thirsty desert air—a spade-foot toad's porous skin can be an asset. Even during the rainy season, spadefoots's skin leaks some water to the air when they surface at night to forage but, when the toads return to their shallow burrows, they rehydrate by absorbing water from the moist soil. After the rainy season the sapitos dig winter burrows as deep as three feet into the soil. As long as the soil stays moist, spadefoots can pull water from it. As the soil dries out however, their spongelike skin becomes a liability. Although spadefoot toads can survive loss of a surprising amount of body water—up to sixty percent, while you or I would be close to death after losing just ten percent of our body weight in water—the parched soil can eventually suck their tissues dry, slowly mummifying the toad in place.

One of spadefoots's antidehydration strategies is to let several outer layers of skin dry out and slough off around their body, forming a desiccation-resistant cocoon. Another is to store water in their bladder, which can hold an amount equal to half of their body weight, as an emergency "canteen." As their outer skin layers dry out, they reabsorb water from their bladder to counteract the effects. But spadefoot toads's most sophisticated strategy involves actually pulling water from the slowly-drying soil through their porous skin into their own tissues. To do this, the sapitos harness a physical property of water called osmosis. Osmosis, from a Greek word meaning "to push," is the tendency of a fluid such as water to pass through a semipermeable membrane, in this case a toad's skin, from the side with a lower concentration of dissolved substances to the side with a higher concentration of dissolved substances. In other words, if the toads can raise the concentration of solutes in their body water above that of the water in the soil, they can pull water molecules in through their skin, thus keeping their body from drying out.

Spadefoots raise the concentration of their body water by storing urea from their urine in the water in their tissues. During the first few months that they are dormant, if the soil contains plenty of water, the toads urinate normally. But as the soil dries out, raising the dissolved solute concentration of the remaining water, the toads stop urinating, instead storing urine in gradually increasing concentrations in their body fluids. (Spadefoot toads can tolerate levels of urea that would kill a human.) In order to survive, sapitos must maintain an equilibrium between the concentration of their body fluids and the increasing tension with which the soil particles grip the remaining water. As long as the water in their body has a higher concentration of dissolved solutes—in this case, urine—than the water in the soil, spadefoots can continue pulling water from the soil into their tissues and keep from dehydrating. All the while that they maintain this delicate balance, the little toads are dormant, their metabolic activity reduced to just a flicker.

When the parents dig themselves into the ground after a hurried night of spadefoot sex, they leave behind egg masses floating in rainwater ponds and puddles. For this new generation of spadefoot toads, the race has just begun. The eggs must hatch and the gilled, aquatic tadpoles must metamorphose into lunged, land-dwelling toads before their ephemeral watery environment vanishes. In order to beat the drying puddles, spadefoot toads race to adulthood much more quickly than most amphibians. Couch's spadefoot eggs can hatch within twenty-four hours and sprint to air-breathing maturity in just over a week! (By comparison, bullfrog tadpoles take two leisurely *years*.) As space and resources grow scarce in their shrinking world, the scores of tiny, black spadefoot tadpoles feed frenziedly on plants and small aquatic animals, and sometimes on each other. In some species, the first tadpoles to hatch secrete a growth inhibitor in their waste that stunts the growth of later hatchlings, giving the oldest the best chance to live and perpetuate the species. In others, tadpoles turn carnivorous, dining on their smaller siblings and cousins, if food becomes scarce. When they have grown sufficiently large to metamorphose into toads, surviving tads emerge from their puddle, gulping air and still dragging their tails.

But they are not ready for the long months of dormancy yet. Although they metamorphose from tadpoles into toads within a few weeks of hatching, the sapitos must feed and grow for several months before they accumulate enough body fat and water to carry them over until the next monsoon season. Vulnerable when they are above ground to predators such as great-tailed grackles, cats, kit foxes, and Gila monsters and to desiccation underground, less than half of the young spadefoot toads will survive to breed the following year.

The spadefoot toads whose bellowing chorus attracted our attention that May night were surfacing in response to the booming thunder. Researchers studying what prompts the small toads's dramatic appearance during summer monsoon thunderstorms discovered that low-frequency sound waves—the sounds of thunder—elicit the mass emergences. Spadefoots dig upwards from their winter depths as soil temperatures warm in the spring and remain close to the surface. A few emerge briefly to forage for food after light rainstorms, but only booming thunder brings out hordes to fill the night with sound. Thunder is apparently the environmental cue most consistently associated with the kind of downpours that elicit termite mating flights *and* produce the puddles and ponds that these sapitos need for mating and egg laying. When spadefoots hear and feel thunder below the soil, they dig upwards, assured that plentiful food and water will greet their emergence. Theirs is an elegant adaptation to water's unpredictable appearance in the desert.

46

Unfortunately, the toads's adaptation has a tragic side. Thunder is not always what it seems. Off-road vehicles used for travel in the desert, especially motorcycles, produce sound waves similar to those of thunder. The booming vibrations of their motors stimulate the small toads to dig to the surface, expending precious calories and moisture. If roused during the dry months—the majority of the year—the little toads find no water, no insects to eat, and they die. Toad researchers worry that heavy off-road vehicle traffic, especially cross-desert motorcycle races like those run in the Mojave Desert of southern California could wipe out local spadefoot toad populations. What an irony that these sapitos, adapted so beautifully to their desert environment, could be deceived and perhaps exterminated by the machines of desert-dwelling humans. Such things make me wonder about our species, named *Homo sapiens*, "wise man."

&

What I love about spadefoot toads—besides their sudden, magical appearance with the first big summer thunderstorms, their equally abrupt disappearance, and their sophisticated adaptations to life in a nearly waterless world—is that these most characteristic indicators of the desert abound in our suburban neighborhood. They link this artificial landscape of neatly trimmed bermuda grass lawns and nonnative shade trees to the desert, bringing wildness back home. The roughly rectangular tract of land that is our subdivision no longer bears much resemblance to desert or tangled bosque. When the subdivision was built in the late 1960s, the developers would never have dreamed of saving any of the original wild tangle: the mesquites and creosote bush and such must have seemed to them like just an untidy patch of weeds. Following the practice of the time, the area was bulldozed and the brush piles burned before the land was filled and divided into neat lots. Tidiness may be next to Godliness in the minds of some people, but not in nature. Our subdivision, with its precisely curving roads and neatly tended yards is certainly tidier than the bosque that it replaced but infinitely less rich and interesting for wild critters.

From the air, our subdivision looks like an island, surrounded by its own moat. Cotton fields lap up to two sides, the grounds of Las Cruces High School touch another side, and an older and distinctly less swanky suburb bounds another side. The irrigation ditch, flanked by a dirt road on each side, runs around the north and east sides of the subdivision like a moat separating this island of urbanity from the rest of the valley. The suburb even stands higher than the surrounding ground. In order to avoid paying flood insurance for this property that is so obviously part of the floodplain of the Río Grande, the developers raised the subdivision by dumping loads of fill on the ground before building the houses. Ironically, the streets still flood after each summer downpour, a reminder of reality.

The high rock and cement block walls completely enclosing the subdivision add to the fortresslike feel. Even the individual lots are divided from each other by four-to-eight-foot-high walls. Each lot—some, like our yard, around a third of an acre in size, most smaller—contains a house, placed approximately in the middle of the lot. The architecture, as in most suburban developments, is startlingly homogenous. The houses are by and large brick, one-story, ranch-style houses, with a two-car garage at one end and three bedrooms at the other end. Except for the Mexican-style ornamental ironwork grilles on many windows and doors, and the occasional cacti, this neighborhood could be anywhere in the United States. The yards are landscaped according to one of two schemes: either an expanse of high-water-use, high-maintenance bermuda grass lawn shaded by spreading mulberry, pecan, or ash trees; or an expanse of low-water-use, low-maintenance gravel dotted with a few, isolated specimens of desert plants. Neither offers much wildlife habitat. There is none of the tangled diversity of the riverbottom woods that once grew here.

Instead of orioles and egrets and yellow-breasted chats and many dozens of other bird species, our subdivision is home to robins—North America's most generic of birds—great-tailed grackles, house finches, English sparrows, and a few other bird species that have adapted to suburban habitat. Instead of tarantulas and scorpions, cockroaches hunt our yards at night. Instead of kit foxes and bobcats, each yard is home to dogs and cats. Many dogs and cats. The results of my informal large pet population census—my thrice-weekly run along the irrigation ditch that borders the backyards of the suburb—shocked me. Nearly each yard that I run by holds a dog or two dogs, or a cat or two cats. From where I meet the ditch road and run north, I pass one yard with no pets, and then a yard with a yapping Chihuahua and a tiger cat that roams free. Past our petless yard, the two bored heel-nipper-type dogs at our neighbors' tear out of the back door to bark at me as I run by. Their two black cats sit on the wall in the sun. Then comes the yard with the two hysterically woofing golden retrievers and a huge tiger Tom and the yard with the large, and very energetic, black lab-German Shepherd cross. Next comes a yard that apparently boasts no domestic animals, followed by a yard with a yapping dog that I have only heard and three big, friendly cats with a fondness for sunning in the ruts of the ditch road. I sometimes stop my run to pet one or the other of them as they wind themselves around my legs, purring loudly. Once I watched with horror as one of the three caught a hummingbird that had stopped to sip nectar from a trumpet-vine flower too close to the ground. Past the cats is the yard with the neurotic German short-haired pointer that doesn't bark but runs laps of the length of the back wall, panting loudly, as I run by. A cat lives there too.

I estimate an average pet population for our subdivision of one per yard. Added to that are the pets that people abandon. Las Cruces Animal Control staff says that the city's cat population is equal to the human population, meaning some sixty thousand cats prowl our town. The dog population, it says, is at least half that. Thirty thousand dogs, sixty thousand cats, and an equal number of humans—It is no wonder that so few of the desert's wild creatures survive here. Not only have we impoverished their habitat, we have simply pushed them out.

Our L-shaped house is typical of the neighborhood: one-story, ranch-style frame structure, red brick facade, and two-car garage facing the street. We are slowly adding a southwestern flavor, enclosing intimate courtyard spaces off of the two main bedrooms, installing skylights and French doors to flood its formerly dark rooms with light, and trading linoleum and carpet on the floors for clay tile. When we bought the house, it was surrounded by a carefully manicured sea of bermuda grass lawn. Two large mulberry trees, one in front and one in back, shaded the yard, producing tons of allergy-inducing pollen each spring. The house is close to the narrow front end of the fan-shaped lot, leaving a large, wedge-shaped backyard. I had originally planned to make the whole yard wild again, killing and rototilling the lawn, cutting down the mulberries, and planting a mix of native plants to approximate the jungle-like bosque that once grew here. The first year, I transformed one whole piece of the backyard into a minibosque, planting mesquite trees over an understory of desert wildflowers, shrubs, and grasses, and building a "hill" at one end studded with native cacti. Unmowed and unwatered, my bosque has grown into a wonderfully wild tangle, with surprises sprouting here and there. The following fall, I killed the bermuda grass lawn in the front yard. My parents came for a weekend and helped me lay thick batts of newspaper on the cornstraw-brittle dead turf, then we covered the newspaper with a pavement of rounded river rocks. Here and there we cut irregular wells through the paper and laid spaghetti-thin irrigation tubes to water infant clumps of desert plants. Now the front is a colorful desert with clusters of shrubs and wildflowers.

I never did cut down the mulberries. Although I sniffle and sneeze for five weeks each spring when they bloom and release their pollen, I've come to love their shade and to value the shelter that they offer for roosting white-winged doves and nesting black-chinned hummingbirds. I'm leaving some lawn in the backyard under the shade of the mulberry there; I've come to appreciate its soothing green oasis. And the flower beds edging the back lawn provide a home to burrowed spadefoot toads.

51

&

That May night of the chorusing toads, when the rain faded to a gentle patter, we took a flashlight and walked through our subdivision in the darkness. The streets were quiet; no lights shined from the other houses. Across El Paseo amidst the rushing traffic, past wet fields that would soon sprout cotton, the sound swelled around us. It seemed to emanate from a normally dry storm water retention basin, a rectangular, several-block area dredged out so that it slopes towards one grassy corner where gapes an eight-foot high grate covering a huge drain culvert. After one of our intense summer thunderstorms, water pours into the grass-covered basin from the parking lots and streets uphill, collecting there rather than flooding the adjacent low ground, including our subdivision.

At the edge of the basin, we shined a flashlight into dark water. Hundreds of small toads floated nearby, their throats swelling and shrinking, swelling and shrinking. We heard both the low trill of southern spadefoot toads and the sheeplike bleat of Couch's spadefoot. I located a trilling sapito in the beam of the flashlight, and we watched it as it floated at the edge of the basin. Behind it the black water rushed by, carrying the detritus of human life, plastic milk jugs, discarded motor oil containers, soda pop bottles, used Pampers, and other debris. Amidst the floating refuse the small toad called with all of its might: First it sucked in air, its belly swelling as if it had swallowed a hockey puck, and then it blew up the pale skin of its throat like a glistening balloon. Finally its mouth opened, producing a high, nasal trill. After a pause, the floating toad gulped in another mighty breath of air, pushed out its glistening throat, and opened its mouth in trilling song again.

52   The city views this place where toads call and mate as just a piece of plumbing, part of the city flood-prevention system, its only purpose being to collect the torrents of water that rush off of city streets and parking lots after thunderstorms. But the toads know it differently. Indeed, located at the eastern edge of the floodplain of the Río Grande, this has always been toad habitat. Originally part of the *bosque*, valleybottom woods, this basin was once shaded by tangles of low, spreading, honey mesquite and *tornillo*—screwbean mesquite—hackberry, and Mexican elder trees. Wavering lines of stately, tall cottonwoods formed a higher canopy here and there, marking the outer edges of the river's successive floods. Orioles wove intricate hanging pouch nests under the cottonwood canopy, Lucy's warblers sang from the mesquites, tiger swallowtails fluttered through the sunny spots between the trees, and deer slipped through the bosque to drink at the river in the evening. And after the summer rains, spadefoot toads emerged to sing and mate in the temporary puddles and ponds.

Humans have lived in this part of the valley for thousands of years without much disturbing the fertile bosques and cienegas. The earliest inhabitants moved around with the seasonal hunting and gathering rhythms, lighting in temporary camps, and augmenting their wild diet with crops from small dry-farmed plantings. By A.D. 900, their descendants had settled along the river in small villages like *Las Tules*, named for nearby cattails. They grew drought-resistant crops such as corn, fished the river for turtles, eels, chub, and sturgeon, hunted large and small animals, built small *pueblos*, and pecked intricate petroglyphs in nearby basalt outcrops. There weren't many humans, and they didn't much alter the face of the valley, an expanse of mesquite bosque, cottonwood forest, and desert shrubland. Sometime after 1450, long-term drought and the arrival of the Apaches, newcomers from the north, made settled agriculture untenable, and they abandoned their crops and their pueblos and returned to a less-comfortable, more-mobile existence.

In 1598, the descendants of these valley dwellers met the caravan of the Spanish explorer/colonizer Don Juan de Oñate near what is now Juárez, Mexico, opening a period of what would be wrenching change for the people of the valley. Within a century, the Spaniards had largely depopulated the valley by forcibly resettling its native population with other Indian groups around missions east of present-day El Paso, Texas, and Juárez, Mexico. The natives died by the scores, killed off by backbreaking work in slavelike conditions, poor food, and introduced diseases. But the bosques and cienegas in this part of the valley remained much the same. Spanish settlement was confined to the *Paso del Norte* area, several days journey to the south.

For the next several hundred years, the little piece of bosque that was to become a storm water retention basin remained quiet, despite important events nearby. The major thorough-fare of the Spanish New World, *El Camino Real*, "The Royal Road" between México City, seat of Spain's New World colony, and Santa Fe, the first capital of New Mexico, the far northern frontier province of Spain and later Mexico, ran right up the Mesilla Valley. All manner of traffic traveled this slow and torturous route. Colonizing parties headed north, led by velvet-clad and plumed-capped aristocrats riding Span-ish horses, and trailed by servants on foot and huge herds of livestock. Army detachments on foot and horseback passed up and down the trail, attempting to impose order on the sprawling territory. Small parties of fur trappers and explor-ers from the then-distant United States traveled south into foreign territory on the sly. Traders's caravans of dozens of slow-moving, wooden-wheeled oxcarts creaked along, car-rying the moveable resources of the province, such as gold, silver, lead, turquoise, hides, and slaves, south to México City, and trade goods north to the frontier. And the Apaches, a mobile hunting, trading, and raiding people who had mi-grated to the region from farther north, darted out of the mountains and mesas to harass the caravans and hunt the fertile valley.

Until the 1840s, the Mesilla Valley, including the future site of the storm water retention basin, served simply as a *paraje*, a stopping place, on the long, dusty Camino Real. Much of northern and central New Mexico had already been parceled out to settlers in land grants first from the king of Spain and then, after independence, from the Mexican gov-ernment. Finally, in 1839, when the farmlands around Paso del Norte had become overcrowded, a group of settlers peti-tioned the Mexican government for land upriver in the Mesilla

Valley. After much bureaucratic consideration, all written out in elegant copperplate script and expressed in flowery Spanish, the 113 would-be colonists were granted the Doña Ana Bend land grant. But by then they were too poor to move and asked that they be allowed a three-year delay to recoup their fortunes. The little group of Mexican settlers finally arrived in the Mesilla Valley in 1843 and founded the settlement of Doña Ana near the northern end of the valley. The colonists immediately commenced digging by hand their all-important, several-mile-long *acequia madre*, literally "mother ditch," to pull water from the wild river to their small fields. Unlike the American system of granting land, much of the hundreds of thousands of acres that comprised the Doña Ana Bend grant were held in common. Only fields and lots in town were parceled out to individual settlers and families; the remainder of the huge land grant, including the piece of bosque that was to become a storm water retention basin, served as communal grazing lands.

55

After the first hard year, when the colony lost most of its members to Apache raids and desertion, the little settlement flourished. But just three years later, the hard-working Mexican colonists found themselves suddenly transferred from Mexico to the United States. The treaty of Guadalupe Hidalgo, signed by Mexico and the United States after the Mexican-American War, abruptly shifted the U.S.–Mexican boundary, once north of what is now Colorado and Utah, hundreds of miles south to near the current border, making much of the Southwest a part of the United States. Thus, the people of the Doña Ana Bend land grant, situated east of the Río Grande, found themselves squarely in the United States, and the land, which they had worked so hard to secure, was now in question. (At that time, the río in Mesilla Valley divided the new United States on the east from Old México on the west.) American arrivals quickly crowded Doña Ana and the valley, squatting wherever they chose on the Mexican settlers's land.

The quiet bosque of this part of the valley probably changed little until nine years later when the new town of Las Cruces was platted several miles south of Doña Ana to keep American settlers and Mexican colonists apart. (Still, Las Cruces sat squarely in the Doña Ana Bend land grant.) What is now a storm water retention basin was then part of the Perfilio Jemente tract, a parcel of land most likely allotted to the Jemente family as part of the Doña Ana Bend grant.

The influx of non-Mexican settlers into the Mesilla Valley after the Mexican-American War changed the landscape of the valley forever. The newcomers, either not understanding or not respecting the system of land grants, simply settled wherever they chose. Some actually purchased their land, but the sellers didn't always own what they sold. Much was community land that could not legally be sold by individuals. (The story was the same when non-Indians flooded reservation land.) The question of the Doña Ana Bend Land Grant colonists's title to their land would not be resolved until nearly sixty years later, when the U.S. Court of Private Land Claims decided in their favor in 1907. Unfortunately, by then many of the original settlers's descendants had already lost their land to fraud, debt, or sale.

In 1849, a group of Mexican colonists moved across the river from Las Cruces to what was still Old México. They founded the town of Mesilla, Little Mesa, on a high spot in the valley west of the Río Grande and secured the Mesilla Civil Colony land grant from the Mexican government in 1853. But just a year later, in 1854, the United States bought the land west of the river as part of the Gadsden Purchase, putting the Mesilleros squarely back in the United States again! And ten years later, the river itself turned on them in a great flood, splitting its channel so that it ran on both sides of Mesilla, isolating the town on an island. Another big flood in 1885 moved the whole river channel from the east side of the valley, where a loop had previously curved along the edge of the Jemente tract, all the way across the valley to west of Mesilla where it now runs.

Although the towns of Las Cruces, Mesilla, and Doña Ana boomed in the first few decades after the Mexican–American war, most of the valley, including the Jemente tract, the current storm sewer basin, remained a rich tangle of bosque and cienega. Mesilla, on the Butterfield Stage Line, the main route to California before railroads and highways, was the center of the region until 1881, when the railroad bypassed it for Las Cruces. After gaining the railroad, Las Cruces soon outpaced the other small towns in the valley, snagging the county seat, and the college that would become New Mexico State University. (The town originally lobbied for the state mental institution and only grudgingly accepted the college instead.) Change was coming to the quiet corner of the bosque. In 1892, fifteen years before the Court of Land Claims at last validated the Doña Ana Bend land grant, the Jemente family lost its tract of bosque to a certain John D. Bryan, in judgment for a debt of $199.75. From then on, the tract remained in Anglo hands.

The completion of Elephant Butte Dam upriver in 1916, with its promise to control floods and irrigate some 175,000 acres of valleybottom land, fired a speculative land boom in the Mesilla Valley. The Jemente tract, as it was still called, changed hands four times in the next fourteen years. During that time, it was probably cleared of its bosque overstory and planted in field crops, alfalfa, grain, and perhaps vegetables. World War II and the testing of the atomic bomb at neighboring White Sands Missile Range brought a boom of another sort to the former bosque—housing developments. The Jemente tract was sold again, this time to a speculator assembling land for a subdivision. Las Cruces remained a small, compact town until World War II. After the explosion of "Fat Man," the first atomic bomb, on White Sands Missile Range in the early morning hours of July 16, 1945, both the weapons research program and Las Cruces boomed. Suburbs spread south towards the university campus, crawled uphill into the desert of East Mesa, and spilled across the farmland to nearly engulf Mesilla and Doña Ana. (The suburb where Richard, Molly, and I live is one of those sprawling developments. It was built in the late 1960s on farm fields that were once mesquite bosque.)

In 1959, Las Cruces bought a piece of the former Jemente tract-turned-subdivision. On part of the purchase were built tennis courts and a swimming pool; the remainder, a two-block-long by one-block-wide rectangle became neighborhood softball fields. But after each big rain, the softball fields flooded several feet deep. The potential for accidental drownings—and the city's liability—soon made city officials nervous. As a result, the former bosque was dredged and turned into a storm water retention basin. For much of each year the grassy basin stands seemingly empty, collecting wind-blown trash while it waits for rain.

Now the old bosque is coming full circle. A community group has "adopted" the retention basin, vowing to replant the bosque and build nature trails to wind through the small area. The group began by planting over fifty trees and shrubs—cottonwoods, desert willows, hackberries and others—during our wet spring.

But the toads always knew. Through all of the changes, colonizing, grazing, bosque-clearing, plowing, subdividing, dredging, and replanting of bosque, the sapitos have reappeared each year to bellow their lust, mate, and gorge on insects.

Their wildness brings the desert home.

The Disappeared Ones

A summer storm reveals the dreaming place of bears.
But you cannot see their shaggy dreams of fish and berries,
any land signs supporting evidence of bears, or any bears at all.
What is revealed in the soaked rich earth, forked waters, and
fence line shared with patient stones is the possibility of
everything you can't see.

Joy Harjo, *Secrets from the Center of the World*

Not long after we moved to this Chihuahuan Desert country, I saw a grizzly bear track. Only grizzly bears don't live here. Everyone knows that.

I had set out for Santa Fe on a clear, sunny September morning, driving an intimate two lane road through Alamogordo, Tularosa, Carrizozo, Corona, Moriarty, and Galisteo rather than the mind-numbing corridor of the interstate highway. On impulse, I turned my car off of the pavement at the old Three Rivers store north of Tularosa, where a sign promising petroglyphs pointed up the gravel road towards the massive ridge of Sierra Blanca. A few miles up the road, I parked my car in a small parking lot and followed a dusty trail up a desert ridge capped with hard volcanic rock.

About halfway up the ridge, I spotted a squiggling line and a circle of dots etched on a dark boulder next to the trail. Nearby, a bat flapped atop another boulder. A little ways away, a larger-than-lifesize human face with almond-shaped eyes stared out over the Tularosa Basin. A coyote, ears perked forward, seemed ready to spring off of the top of another boulder. Across another dark rock swam a fat fish, its checkered sides suggesting scales. The more I looked, the more petroglyphs I saw. Many boulders contained several petroglyphs; others only one. Some drawings were big; others so small that I had to search carefully to find them. I wandered the undulating ridgeline, finding hundreds of vivid, lively drawings.

Rounding one group of boulders, I looked down and sucked in my breath, startled by what I saw. There, etched in the rock, was a clear footprint of a grizzly bear, its pale outline contrasting sharply with the dark desert varnish. It was a hind foot, longer than my hand from the bear's rounded heel to its wickedly curved claws. I'd seen a lot of grizzly footprints when I worked in their territory in northwest Wyoming. I had no doubt about this print—it was clearly that of a grizzly. But I had never imagined grizzlies here. I studied the rock drawing carefully. When I looked up, my view took in the whole Tularosa Basin, a thousand square miles of desert scrubland shimmering in the intense sunlight, blue hazy and level as the lake bed that it once was, stretching south to Old México. Grizzlies here?

Indeed. Nor am I alone in my ignorance. Most residents of southern New Mexico have forgotten that grizzlies once inhabited this parched landscape, and not so long ago. The last known grizzly bear in southern New Mexico was killed in the Mogollon Mountains in 1931. A century ago, grizzlies were common in these parts. Biologists estimate that several thousand grizzlies roamed the Southwest's grasslands, oak and piñon-juniper woodlands, and pine forests from the *sierras* in Sonora and Chihuahua, México, north to the small island mountain ranges studding the Colorado Plateau in southern Utah. Letters, journals, tall tales, rituals, and stories of the Southwest are populated by the big bears.

The earliest mention of grizzlies in the Chihuahuan Desert region by Anglo travelers came in 1824, when James Ohio Pattie, a mountain man traveling downriver along the Río Grande near present-day Socorro, New Mexico—not a place that brings grizzlies to mind today—reported in his journal, "We saw great numbers of bears, deer and turkeys." David E. Brown, author of *The Grizzly in the Southwest*, and other biologists count these as grizzlies because the riverbottom cottonwood forest was prime grizzly, not black bear, habitat. After a bear chased one of his party into camp, Pattie says baldly, "We killed it." Its fate presaged that of its fellows.

After the boom brought about by the Civil War, the eastern states plunged into an economic bust. The federal government, hoping to spark another boom, advertised the West to settlers, promising free land under the Homestead Act and conveniently ignoring the native peoples who had long ago "settled" the whole West. Floods of migrants poured in, bringing with them millions of cows, sheep, horses, and goats. The army, with thousands of idle soldiers to occupy, began a new war, this time on Native Americans. Army forts and camps popped up in wild country all across the West, bringing their own grazing livestock. At the same time, news of silver and gold strikes began luring flocks of hopeful prospectors to the Southwest. Boomtown mining camps sprouted quickly. Grizzlies, not yet wary of humans, were irresistible targets for anyone with a gun.

But it was cattle that sealed southwestern grizzlies's fate. *Criollos*, or Spanish cattle, had arrived in what is now northern México and the southern Southwest with Francisco

Coronado's expedition in 1540. In 1598, Don Juan de Oñate's train of colonists trailed seven thousand head of livestock north from Chihuahua, México to found Santa Fe, the first European capital in North America. By the time that Lieutenant Colonel Philip St. George Cooke and his five hundred Mormon volunteers blazed a wagon road across the Chihuahuan Desert in southwestern New Mexico in 1846, huge herds of feral criollos roamed nearby in northern México. Still, it was not until the 1880s, boom years for the cattle business in the United States Southwest, that cattle flooded the range of the grizzlies here. Between 1882 and 1884, *sixty thousand* cattle were moved into Socorro Country, New Mexico alone, an area that now supports much less than one-tenth that number. High cattle prices and the apparent high productivity of the desert grasslands encouraged ranchers to graze wildly optimistic numbers of livestock. The grass seemed endless, the profits sure.

Unfortunately, the ranchers were mistaken on both counts. By the middle of the 1880s, the effects of overuse had begun to show. Grasslands once described as knee-high on a horse developed bare spots like a carpet worn to the backing. Spring wind storms scoured away tons of topsoil where the grass no longer rooted it. Cattle prices crashed. Nearly two years of drought followed, exacerbating the degradation. In 1886, for the first time, more cattle were shipped out of the Southwest than in. Then came two years of higher rainfall. Struggling ranchers increased their herds in an attempt to recoup earlier losses. The rainfall soon turned into a curse. The newly bared landscape could no longer soak up and store the moisture like a sponge; instead, water ran off in sheets, carrying the soil with it. Old photographs show staggering devastation:

Raw, steep-walled gullies gouge the once-flat surfaces of over-grazed mountain meadows; arroyos cut down into once-gentle desert streambeds, leaving lines of cottonwoods high and dry; everywhere the landscape looks bare and worn. In 1891, the price of beef plummeted again, followed by the drought of 1891–1893, the worst yet. Cattle starved or died of thirst. In southcentral Arizona alone, at least 350,000 head of cattle and perhaps more than a million, died. Cattle carcasses were so thick, according to contemporary accounts, that a person could throw a rock from one carcass to the next across that vast landscape. More than half of the cattle herds in the Southwest perished.

For the next decade, droughts alternated with wet years, and cattle prices fluctuated with a boom-bust cycle. Intent on making "good use" of every last bit of the range, ranchers added sheep to browse the shrubs inedible to cattle, and Angora goats to crop the steepest slopes and rugged high country that other stock would not graze.

The grass seemed endless, the profits sure.

The effects on the Southwest's "endless" supply of native forage are visible still. It is difficult now, a hundred years later, to imagine the pre-1880s desert landscapes. Conjure up, in your mind's eye, clumps and mats of dry grass spreading across areas where today's hard-as-adobe, bare desert soil, studded with sparse shrubs, no longer brings "grassland" to mind. Imagine the sparkle of water in long-disappeared *cienegas*— marshes—brought alive by red-winged blackbirds's musical calls and the whistle of hundreds of duck wings. Picture braided desert rivers chortling year-round, home to Chihuahua chub and other desert fish, where now bone dry arroyos bake in the sun.

The cycle of overgrazing and drought was devastating to Southwest grizzlies. Although they are omnivorous, grizzly bears are dependent on "salad stuff," bulbs, tubers, roots, succulent stems and leaves, berries, and nuts. The big bears also eat carrion, fish, grassland rodents, and insects such as ants and grubs. Over the course of a year, Southwest grizzlies ranged from mountain forests to desert, following the available food in a distinct seasonal pattern from their springtime emergence from high-country dens to winter's hibernation. Then overgrazing, combined with logging of whole watersheds for mine timbers, railroad ties, and wood to fuel mine smelters, decimated grizzlies's landscapes and their traditional food sources. The big bears began to die off.

Still, the Southwest's grizzlies might have survived. A growing conservation ethic in the early 1900s spurred the creation of national forests, parks, and national monuments on public land in the Southwest. Wildlife managers like Aldo Leopold began working to save the remaining populations of other big wild animals: black bears, pronghorn antelope, elk, moose, and mule and white-tailed deer. But big predators like grizzlies, wolves, mountain lions, and jaguars were not among the chosen. Pressured by habitat degradation and human encroachment, the big bears often turned to the new, easily available food sources, cows, sheep, and other livestock. Grizzlies were branded dangerous, inimical to "civilized" settlement. They became public enemy number one. To kill a grizzly in the Southwest at the time was to strike a blow for civilization, for God and country, a public service worthy of a hero's commendation. While government-paid wildlife managers labored to nurse other species back from the brink of extinction, government-paid trappers and hunters killed off the Southwest's grizzlies.

It didn't take long. In the late 1920s, U.S. Biological Survey experts estimated that at least forty-eight grizzly bears still lived in the remote mountains and high mesas of eastern Arizona and western New Mexico. It turns out that they were wrong. The last grizzly in New Mexico was shot on Rain Creek in the Mogollon Mountains of the extreme western part of the state just three years later; the last grizzly in Arizona was killed in 1935 by two government trappers, one of whom, quoted by Brown in *The Grizzly in the Southwest*, said later that if he'd known it was the last grizzly, he would never have killed the big bear. Such is hindsight.

The grass seemed endless, the profits sure.

In just fifty years, grizzlies were exterminated in the American Southwest. Once considered inexhaustible like the grass in desert grasslands, the big bears disappeared so fast that there was not even time to take their scientific measurements, to gather data, to describe them. Early accounts confuse the record by calling grizzlies by many different names. Some refer to grizzlies as "cinnamon bears" for their variegated fur or "white bears" for the pale hair tips that give a silvery sheen to their hump-backed shape. Others called the big bears *el oso plateado*, "the silver bear," *el oso gris*, "the gray bear," or simply *el oso*, "the bear," a tribute to their commanding size and temper. Whatever their name, so few specimens remain of the Southwest's thousands of grizzlies that biologists can only speculate about how different they were from their Rocky Mountain cousins.

Our Southwestern bears were among the most southerly of grizzly populations around the world. Some biologists speculate that the grizzlies of the Southwest's mountains and the Colorado Plateau were probably a different race from the

"Plains grizzlies" of the southern Southwest and northern México and that both were different still from the also-exterminated California grizzlies and the still-surviving Rocky Mountain grizzlies. Unfortunately, too little information remains to tell us how or if Southwestern grizzlies differed from their kin. Were our grizzlies really bigger as contemporary accounts suggest? With food available more of the year, did our grizzlies hibernate for fewer months? In these sparsely-vegetated landscapes, did our osos have larger ranges than the up-to-180-square-mile home ranges of Rocky Mountain silvertips? We cannot know. Except for the stories and the long-clawed footprints chipped into the rock, they are gone.

Their ghosts persist though. Grizzlies lived in the relatively remote mountains of northern México until at least the early 1960s. A big male oso killed in Chihuahua's Sierra del Nido in 1960 by a trophy-hunting dentist from Chihuahua City is one of the best documented of the Southwest's grizzlies and was thought to be the last. Then, in the fall of 1979, a hunting guide killed a sixteen-year-old female grizzly near the head of the Navajo River in southern Colorado's San Juan Mountains. He says that she attacked him; the existing evidence, at best, muddies the story. Encouraged by signs that she had nursed cubs and by continuing reports of grizzly sign—hair, tracks, diggings, and such—in the San Juans, some believe that a few of the big bears still hang on there in the extreme northern Southwest. Others pin their hopes on continuing rumors that *el oso* persists in the Sierra Madre of northern Sonora, Mexico.

Grizzlies survive in other ways also. Images of the big bears populate southwestern folklore and art; their presence permeates traditional beliefs. In *Juan Oso*, Texas folklorist and historian J. Frank Dobie recounts several versions of a *cuento*, folktale, starring grizzlies, in which a big male *encantado*, or enchanted, bear steals a beautiful young Mejicana woman to live with him. In some cuentos she is kidnapped on the eve of her wedding and later rescued by her frantic human kin; in other cases, she bears her captor/lover a grizzly-human son, *Juan Oso*. The cuentos often include detailed knowledge of southwestern grizzlies, their diets, their haunts, and the habits of their days. They also reveal a respect for the big bears. In Dobie's *Juan Oso*, the storyteller says, "The bear is more like a man than any other animal. He can walk upright; he has hands to use; he eats the same food that *cristianos* eat; his brain is quick to understand."

Southwest Native American tradition, too, considers humans and bears to be closely related. (A skinned bear looks eerily like a human form.) Although traditions differ between various groups, all view bears as serious "medicine," creatures possessing great powers. Many traditional Native Americans are careful to refer to the big bears obliquely rather than by their true name, thus avoiding disturbing their powerful spirits. Mescalero Apaches, for instance, speak of bears as *Kanteol*, broad foot, rather than the name for bear. Although most Southwest Native American traditions forbid the killing of the big bears because of their close connection to humans and their great power, certain Pueblo and Navajo clans have ceremonial bear-hunting cults. Grizzly claws, feet, and hides are still considered important medicine and are carefully preserved for certain ceremonies.

Grizzly bears flourish, too, in contemporary southwestern images. Grizzly-bear footprints march across t-shirts, ball caps, belt buckles, money clips, and key rings; bears decorate silver

69

button covers, earrings, bolo ties, pins, and other jewelry; stylized bears appear on posters, in paintings, on pottery, as fetishes, and in other art.

Why this continuing fascination with bears in general and grizzlies in particular? Perhaps bears are just another southwestern fad, like howling coyotes. I like to think that the attraction is deeper than that. I think that our fascination with osos in literature, art, and life stems from an unconscious understanding that grizzlies belong here. Their wild *animas*, or soul, is an essential part of the Southwest. I feel cheated by the absence of grizzly bears in this Chihuahuan Desert country. Living and working around grizzlies for many years in the backcountry of Wyoming taught me respect for the big bears and changed my attitude toward nature in general. Some wild animals adapt to human habitat, modifying their behavior to fit in with people. Not grizzlies. They, wolves, and a few other animals, are the conscience of wildness. Grizzlies require wild country and tolerate human intrusion only if we remember that we are small enough to constitute food. While doing fieldwork in their wilderness, I learned to adapt to their rules, fit into their territory, and not to insist that they and the country change to suit me. I worked with my senses alert, in the constant awareness of the presence of big, powerful bears. I once watched, safely from the opposite side of a wide and deep river, a yearling grizzly gallop smoothly as a racehorse across a meadow at about thirty-five miles per hour. It leapt graceful despite its three-hundred-pound bulk, into the air after a sandhill crane, like a dog chasing magpies. The crane flew away unhurt; the bear thudded back to earth. That kind of wild grace has no equal. Without grizzlies, a landscape is impoverished, less rich, less vital.

I think, too, that our fascination with the big bears comes from a biological truth, a nearly forgotten memory of what grizzlies mean to this country. Grizzlies were an indicator, a barometer of sorts, of our effect on the Southwest. Had we been paying attention as their populations crashed, they could have taught us something. Like the canary in the mine tunnel or the salmon in the Pacific Northwest, their shrinking numbers were a warning. The demise of grizzlies told the story of what enthusiastic exploitation of the Southwest's desert grasslands, mineral resources, woodlands, and forests did to the landscape: depleted it. In overusing grizzlies's preferred habitats, the stream and riverside cottonwood forests, the grasslands, the piñon-juniper and oak woodlands, and the mountain meadows, we injured the whole region—human habitat also. Those heady decades, when the grasslands seemed endless, the profits sure, left us all poorer. What we inhabit now is a diminished Southwest, faded like a picture left out in the sun so long that its exquisite details blur and disappear, a Southwest with fewer species, less water, a seemingly barren place. Only in the past few decades have biologists begun to realize what we are missing and to reconstruct what the Southwest looked like when grizzlies still roamed this landscape.

When the grass seemed endless, the profits sure.

In the late 1940s, nearly three decades after he left the Southwest, Aldo Leopold wrote "Escudilla," an essay about the killing of Bigfoot, a lone grizzly on Escudilla Mountain in eastcentral Arizona. Although the big bear "claimed for his own only a cow a year and a few square miles of useless rocks," Leopold says, "his personality pervaded the county." That is until progress arrived in the form of the government trapper who, after many attempts, finally bagged Bigfoot. Only after the grizzly was gone, his pelt carted off, and his skull sent to the National Museum did Leopold and his land management cronies begin to wonder if eliminating Bigfoot truly constituted progress. Not until the big bear was gone did they recognize him as a crucial part of the Southwest. Then, too late, they mourned the old grizzly and the wild spirit that he brought to the landscape. Leopold's closing lines stick in my heart: "Escudilla," he wrote, "still hangs on the horizon, but when you see it you no longer think of bear. It's only a mountain now."

☙

The afternoon that I first visited Three Rivers, I wandered among the petroglyphs on the boulder-strewn ridgetop until the slanting sunlight recalled the time. Afterward, I hurried back down the ridge to the car, drove the dusty gravel road to the highway, and headed north. To this day, those petroglyphs, powerful, lively images evoking the spirit of this desert landscape, haunt me.

They stick with me because of their spirit and because the drawings depict an extraordinarily diverse multitude of Chihuahuan Desert lives: bats, tadpoles, owls, eagles, swifts, grasshoppers, coyotes, butterflies, fish, toads, lizards, snakes, bighorn sheep, pronghorn antelope, jackrabbits, beetles. All are in motion. They dance, prance, fly, swim, or leap from nearly every rock. The simple, startlingly contemporary style of the petroglyphs infuses each animal with life. The cumulative effect of the drawings is one of an abundance of exuberant, fascinating lives. Not harshness, not desolation, not alienation. The petroglyphs at Three Rivers seem to represent an attitude towards this "barren, wild, and worthless"

Chihuahuan Desert that no longer prevails: joy. The people who created these drawings must have *loved* this desert. There is no sense of the desert as the "other"; these images come from a people who are part of this desert.

When I first saw the petroglyphs at Three Rivers, I felt that I'd found ancestors—if not genetic forbearers, then ancestors of the heart. These seemed to be people whose attitude towards this difficult landscape was what I wished for: one of kinship to the desert and its other inhabitants, not of subduing or fighting it; one of celebrating the sacred in the Chihuahuan Desert and its lives, large and small, common and rare. It seemed that they saw the desert, as Aldo Leopold hoped we would, as "a community to which we belong," not a "commodity belonging to us." I wanted to know these people.

73

Their story is fragmented and blurry, worn thin by the distance of years. They are less well known even than the Southwest's grizzly bears. The brief interpretive signs at Three Rivers say only that the rock drawings were chiseled between a thousand and six hundred years ago, while Europe endured the latter half of the Middle Ages, by a people whom archaeologists call the Jornada Mogollon. The Mogollon inhabited the northern Chihuahuan Desert region throughout southern New Mexico, southeastern Arizona, west Texas, and northern México. Unlike their contemporaries, the Anasazi of the Colorado Plateau and the Hohokum of Arizona's Sonoran Desert, the Chihuahuan Desert–dwelling Mogollon left few striking architectural remains. Only their extraordinary art—black-on-white Mimbres pottery produced for a brief period in southwestern New Mexico and the haunting rock drawings throughout the Chihuahuan Desert region—

reaches through the centuries to touch our hearts and minds. Images from Mogollon art have become synonymous with "southwestern" art: modern Pueblo artists borrow the lively animal and human figures to decorate pottery and jewelry; the images frolic on t-shirts, pot holders, posters, and other art and design. But the culture that produced this now-popular art remains anonymous.

The creators of the petroglyphs at Three Rivers most likely lived in villages strung along now-dry Three Rivers Creek. But their story begins centuries earlier. Their ancestors, a hunting-gathering culture named the Chihuahua Archaic by archaeologists, were among the first wave of people to settle the Southwest near the end of the Glacial Age some fifteen thousand years ago. (Some researchers now think that people may have begun arriving much earlier.) Paul Martin of the Desert Laboratory in Tucson thinks that these few thousand hunter-gatherers were responsible for the first wave of extinctions on the North American continent. Martin and others think that these skilled hunters left the Siberian Plains because that landscape was overpopulated and hunted out. Arriving in the North American Southwest, they found what must have seemed the Promised Land indeed. The Southwest at that time was dominated by a group of enormous, plant-eating animals—mastodons, giant camels, huge ground sloths, armadillos the size of Volkswagen Beetles, and others—that had evolved without human predation. Like the Southwest's grizzlies before the 1850s, the king-sized plant-eaters had no experience with two-legged humans and so didn't know their deadly potential. About eleven thousand years ago, all traces of these huge mammals disappear. If Paul Martin and his colleagues are correct, the Siberian immigrants exploited these giant-sized meals-on-the-hoof so enthusiastically that, in a short few thousand years, they killed off the entire Pleistocene fauna of mega-animals, some fifty-five species in all. Each little band of hunters no doubt reassured themselves that there were so few humans and so many mastodons, camels, ground sloths, and giant armadillos that this resource would surely last forever.

The grass seemed endless, the profits sure.

With the Pleistocene mega-animals gone, the Chihuahua Archaic peoples were forced to change their food-gathering technology from killing huge animals and then feasting on the abundance to a lifestyle that could be supported on the remaining smaller game and on wild plant foods. This involved learning a very detailed knowledge of the desert's natural resources, what plants and animals could be eaten, how and where to catch or harvest them, and when they were most easily obtained. Their lives revolved around seasonal migrations based on harvesting the desert's foods, from bighorn sheep to agave hearts. Then, some four thousand years ago—around three thousand years before the first petroglyphs were chipped into the rocks at Three Rivers—the Chihuahua Archaic acquired corn and the techniques to cultivate it from México. (Corn, a wild grass with large grains, had been cultivated in México since at least 7000 B.C.)

At first, the new technology of agriculture didn't change these hunter-gatherers's lives much. They simply planted corn kernels in locations where the plants might grow and continued on their seasonal migrations, returning later in the year to harvest whatever corn had survived the summer and had remained uneaten by insects and other animals. Gradually, however, the Chihuahua Archaic societies learned more sophisticated horticultural methods and began to make greater use of this new food. As they did, their lives and culture subtly changed. They paid more attention to their seasonal plantings, and they settled for longer periods of time, imperceptibly becoming more like farmers and less like wandering opportunists.

Over centuries, the Chihuahua Archaic peoples saved and replanted kernels from their most successful crops, eventually breeding varieties of corn that would thrive and produce ever-larger ears in their local climates. At the same time and also from cultures farther south in what is now México, they learned the art of digging clay and shaping and firing it into pottery. The gradual adoption of the two technologies revolutionized life for the Archaic peoples: Pottery allowed them to carry water, slowcook food, and store seeds for long periods of time; with corn they could grow a dependable food supply instead of relying solely on the often-undependable provenance of the desert.

By around A.D. 400, the new technologies enabled the once-nomadic Chihuahua Archaic peoples to settle down. In the process, their culture gradually metamorphosed into the agricultural, village-oriented culture that archaeologists named the Mogollon, the first southwesterners to farm and shape pots and to build permanent dwellings, earth-sheltered structures called pithouses. As corn, pottery, and pithouse architecture spread through the Southwest, these new agriculturists changed other cultures, beginning a revolution on the order of Europe's Industrial Revolution. These technologies gave us the Anasazi, who built their cliffhouse cities and pueblo complexes at Mesa Verde, Chaco Canyon, and elsewhere; the Hohokum, who built sprawling towns with sunken ball courts and who engineered hundreds of miles of irrigation ditches to water extensive farms in the Sonoran Desert; and the Mogollon, whose art endures. Populations grew, trade flourished, prosperity ruled.

It was after the corn-pottery-pithouse revolution that the petroglyph artists at Three Rivers incised their drawings on the windswept ridge. Beginning in about A.D. 1000, the villages boomed. New houses were built above ground with stone foundations and adobe walls. The villagers farmed the bottomlands of the valley, raising corn, beans, and squash. They hunted and gathered wild foods. They shaped pottery decorated with graceful geometric designs. And, like today's catalog shoppers, the Three Rivers Mogollon traded. Itinerant Aztec merchants or *pochteca* from the trading city of Paquimé, near Casas Grandes, many days walk to the south in what is now northern México brought them bright macaw feathers, copper bells, animal fetishes, stone balls and such in return for pottery, wild plant foods, and other natural resources. Life was relatively good.

But not for long. Sometime between A.D. 1350 and 1450, the boom went bust—big time. The Mogollon abruptly abandoned their villages at Three Rivers and throughout the northern Chihuahuan Desert region, leaving almost everything behind. The ruins contain tools, pots, and the usual household goods, but no people. There is no evidence of disease, warfare, or other conflict; they left behind no hasty burials, no mass graves, no sign of chaos, no piles of weapons. The Mogollon seem to have simply walked away from their houses and fields and vanished into the creosote bush desert or the dark conifer forest of the mountains.

Throughout the Southwest, the story is the same: By the

close of the fourteenth century, the neighboring Anasazi (in Navajo, roughly, the ancient ones or the disappeared ones) had left their multistoried cities at Chaco Canyon, Mesa Verde, and elsewhere. Southern Arizona's Hohokum had abandoned their adobe towns, ball courts, and extensive irrigation projects. The Aztec traders had left the city of Paquimé in northern Chihuahua with its hundreds of apartments, plazas, and its ultramodern stone-lined water supply system.

What happened? Dendrochronology, the study of tree growth rings, provides an important clue. Southwestern trees dating back to that time show narrowed growth rings, evidence of serious drought. Instead of droughts coming every two or three years on average, the trees say that gradually, the norm shifted to a dry year every other year. Then, in the late 1200s, the pencil-line-thin tree rings say that the rains simply quit coming. One exceptionally dry year followed another, and another, and another for at least twenty-five years. Crops failed, year after year after hungry year. Hunters traveled farther and farther to search for scarcer game or to harvest smaller and smaller yields of wild plant foods. Many archaeologists believe that the long drought decimated human populations throughout the Southwest. At first, archaeologists assumed that the Mogollon, like the Anasazi, the Hohokum, and the *pochteca* of Paquimé, simply disappeared after a natural catastrophe.

The story is not that simple. New evidence shows that the catastrophic drought wasn't entirely natural. The Mogollon and the Southwest's other cultures made it worse. The very technologies that enabled them to settle and flourish also enabled population growth and enthusiastic resource exploitation. As village populations grew and trade increased, the Southwest's peoples stripped the landscape around their villages and cities, harvesting all of the nearby firewood, timber, wild game, and plant foods, the way that large colonies of harvester ants strip the area bare around their mound. For the Three Rivers people, expanding populations meant growing more food, killing more wild game, gathering more wild plants. More people also meant more houses and therefore more trees cut for house roof beams, more rocks for foundations, and more earth mined for adobe bricks. Trade with the pochteca meant producing more pottery: digging more clay, using more water, and harvesting more firewood to fuel kilns. Eventually, "more" was simply too much for the desert.

We now know that denuding the landscape, whether by stripping forests and woodlands of their tree cover or grazing grasslands down to bare soil, creates "heat islands." Bare soil absorbs more of the sun's heat than unbared areas, dries out more quickly, and thus stores and reflects more heat back into the air. Rain comes in part from moisture in the local soil. The drier the soil, the less life-giving moisture it transmits back to the air. Removing the forest cover, or the grass cover—or creating large areas of pavement, as we do in today's cities and urban areas—can thus heat up and dry out the climate, changing a landscape from a nurturing place to a desolate one.

Like the enthusiastic miners, loggers, and ranchers of the pre-1930s Southwest, or like the rapidly growing populations of today's Southwest, the Mogollon seem to have borrowed beyond the desert's ability to produce. They thus depleted the Chihuahuan Desert region's slender but once-adequate inventory of natural resources, the very resources on which they themselves lived.

The grass seemed endless, the profits sure.

How could people who overused the desert have produced

the petroglyphs at Three Rivers, those extraordinarily lively depictions of fish, birds, bats, insects, rain clouds? How could they have produced powerful images that seem to celebrate the desert environment, while living as they did?

According to the interpretive signs at Three Rivers, the drawings's purpose is not clear. Perhaps, the authors of the signs say, the ridge may have been a lookout site for hunting, implying that the thousands of images peopling the rocks are doodles pecked by bored hunters as they waited for suitable game. Or the ridge may have lain along a well-traveled route, implying that these powerful designs are ancient graffiti on the order of "Juan Y Cruz—Amor Siempre" or "Northside Rules." But petroglyph-carving is slow, hard work. Having tried my hand at it and spent hours trying to chip one line into the hard rock, I doubt if the deceptively simple petro-glyphs are frivolous. I like the final suggestion by the authors of the signs: The area, they say, might have had religious significance.

I think that the petroglyphs are prayers.

Imagine that the rains come less and less frequently, your crops shrivel, and the desert yields less food. Hunger haunts your every day. You are afraid. You appeal to the desert that once nurtured you, squatting on the ridgetop for hours, days. You carefully peck drawings into the dark rocks, etching them with prayers for rain, for life, for the return of the desert's blessing. For a return to a time when the grass seemed endless, the profits sure.

If the petroglyphs were prayers, they were not answered.

The Three Rivers people and others throughout the Southwest fled their villages, leaving behind everything. What happened to them? Did these people, like the Southwest's grizzly bears, really disappear?

No. The Mogollon culture may have disappeared, but the people didn't, although many no doubt died. Faced with starvation, the Mogollon, the Anasazi, the Hohokum, and the *pochteca* of Paquimé adapted. They abandoned now-insupportable large settlements with their fancy houses and their consumer goods, split up into smaller groups, and resettled in much simpler, lower-tech settlements near reliable water sources such as the Río Grande. Despite their evolution of comparatively high-technology lifestyles, the Mogollon still knew how to survive in this arid country. Their sophisticated knowledge of the desert environment shows in the location and design of their fields, in the layout of their villages, in the variety of wild plants that they harvested and animals that they hunted, and in the petroglyphs that they chipped into the rocks at Three Rivers. Like their ancestors the Chihuahua Archaic, the Mogollon knew where the perennial springs were, when edible bulbs could be dug in mountain meadows, when the yucca fruits ripened, and how to efficiently hunt bighorn sheep. Their ancestors had survived in the desert for centuries, living in small groups and moving with the food. Theirs was not an easy way to live, but it served. The Mogollon apparently had not forgotten that technology. They most likely inherited it in the form of stories and rituals and, with that information, knew how to survive the long years of drought. But in the doing, they had to change their culture radically, giving up their settled existence, their stone houses, their trade goods, and their irrigated farms.

Where did the Three Rivers people go? Not far. Research by Patrick H. Beckett and Terry L. Corbett links these Mogollon people to several of the Indian groups encountered by the Spaniards in the Río Grande valley two centuries after the catastrophic drought near what are now El Paso and Las Cruces. Among these people were the *Manso*, or peaceful ones, a group named by Don Juan de Oñate in 1598, according to his journals, because their first words were "*manxo, manxo, micos, micos*, by which they meant 'peaceful ones and friends.'" The Manso, mistakenly thought to be Apaches, who were relative newcomers to the Southwest, lived along the river in the Río Grande valley from what is now Elephant Butte Reservoir in New Mexico south to a few miles below El Paso, Texas. Unlike their Mogollon ancestors's villages of permanent adobe and stone dwellings, the Manso lived near the river in *rancherías*, small clusters of simple dwellings described as straw (probably reeds and cattails) or brush shelters. The Manso fished and hunted, gathered wild plant foods, and farmed small plots of corn, squash, and beans like their Mogollon forbearers. Despite what the Spaniards described as "squalid conditions," the peaceful ones lived as well as the slender resources of the desert allowed. They welcomed the often-half-starved Spanish travelers, treating them to feasts of corn, mesquite beans, and fish of many kinds.

The Spaniards did not reciprocate in kind. In an effort to convert the Manso—a well-intentioned idea that nevertheless proved disastrous—the Mission of Nuestra Señora de Guadalupe de Los Mansos was established in what is now Juárez, México in 1659. In 1667, the Manso building the mission church, apparently tired of mission life, revolted. The local *alcalde*, Captain Andres de Gracia, put down the rebellion and hung the two Manso leaders. For the remainder of the 1600s, the "peaceful" Manso sporadically rebelled. After the Pueblo Rebellion that caused the Spaniards to retreat from northern New Mexico in 1680, the population of the missions in El Paso swelled with loyal Pueblo Indians who had retreated south with the defeated Spaniards. The crowded conditions fueled one last Manso rebellion. A whole group of Manso escaped and lived free in the Franklin Mountains above Paso del Norte, accompanied by other Chihuahuan Desert–dwelling Native American groups, also probable descendants of the Mogollon. But by 1698, the Spaniards had subdued them all and corralled them into area missions.

By the early nineteenth century it seemed as if the Manso, descendants of the "vanished" Mogollon, themselves had disappeared. Life at the Spanish missions was not easy. Crowded conditions, European diseases, and a strange diet decimated their population; "re-education" by the Spanish padres and intermarriage with other Indian groups blurred languages and cultures. When anthropologist Adolph Bandelier came to Paso del Norte in the 1880s to document the cultures of the Indian groups there, he found neither speakers of the Manso language nor traces of their culture. It seemed that they too were gone.

Like their ancestors the Mogollon and the Southwest's grizzlies, the Manso did not vanish. Their descendants live on in area pueblos, including the village of Tortugas just south of Las Cruces. The community was settled in the mid-1880s by a small group of people descended from the various Indian groups forced into the missions of Paso del Norte. Although nearly forgotten by the outside world, the little village of Tortugas has survived. By most measures of economic success, it is a poor place, but it is rich in culture. Like the Mogollon and Manso before them, the tightly knit community has evolved a new culture partly based on its old traditions; it has changed in order to survive in a changing world.

Today, the village of Tortugas considers itself neither strictly

83

an Indian pueblo nor a traditional Hispanic community. Each December, the village celebrates its mixed Mejicano and Indian ancestry and reaffirms its bond to its home landscape with a fiesta in honor of the *Virgen de Guadalupe*, the brown-skinned Virgin who appeared to a Mexican Indian in the 1500s on the site of a former Aztec temple. The three-day festival draws crowds of Tortugas residents home from however far they have wandered and crowds of nonresidents who come to share in the traditions. The fiesta, which requires months of preparation, includes processions of the image of Our Lady—as the *Virgen de Guadalupe* is affectionately called—an all-night prayer vigil, Indian-and Aztec-inspired dance groups, and a day-long pilgrimage up nearby Tortugas Mountain that culminates in a spectacular, bonfire-lit descent. The fiesta serves to tie the community together, to reinforce its evolving culture. It reminds the residents of Tortugas, whether the rest of the world notices or not, that they have not, indeed, disappeared.

ॐ

One July, a hailstorm pounded our neighborhood, destroying most of the house roofs including ours. Since we had to replace our roof, we decided to do other remodeling at the same time. Over the weeks that construction crews worked on our house, we became friends with the contractor. He stopped to talk each time he visited, answering my questions about Las Cruces and telling me tidbits about the neighborhoods and the people of his childhood. As I pieced them together, they gave a new dimension to the Mogollon-Manso-Tortugas story.

Our contractor, Carlos Sanchez, is a big man, tall and barrel-chested, with rich mahogany-colored skin, black eyes, and wavy, raven's-feather-black hair. He looks like a classic example of a *mestizo*, half-Indian, half-Hispanic. Indeed he is: his mother is the daughter of the last hereditary *cacique*, or headman, of Tortugas pueblo and a descendent of those "disappeared" Mansos; his father is a blue-eyed, blond-haired Hispano, who could, if he chose, pass for an Anglo. Carlos's father's family, dismayed when Carlos's father began hanging around with "that Roybal girl," told him to stay away from "those Indians." With his Anglo looks, Carlos's father could have married well according to his family's definition, but he persisted and married Carlos's mother. Love did not immediately overcome familial prejudice. For years, Carlos says, his father's family, the Sanchezes, refused to accept Carlos's mother and her family, simply because the Roybals were Indians. Carlos says regretfully that he didn't learn to speak the Tiwa language of his mother's family when he was growing up "because of the prejudice."

Now in his forties, Carlos is especially conscious of the loss of his Tiwa Indian heritage. He wishes, he says, that he had learned the traditions that make it special, give it an identity, and root it in this landscape. He and other Tortugas Indians, a group that split off from the village of Tortugas, have applied to the federal government for official recognition as a living—not disappeared—Indian tribe. But the group is struggling, split by political and personal differences. Many of the stories that once defined the community have been lost. It is difficult to recover or reinvent a culture when you no longer have a clear sense of what that culture is.

Carlos Sanchez grew up in the old *barrio*, the original Latino neighborhoods just east of downtown Las Cruces. The neighborhood of his childhood embraced the old downtown: his uncle's hardware store, a long, narrow building between Church and Campo Streets; and the square block occupied by Saint Genevieve's, the Catholic church, with its spreading churchyard and outbuildings. Carlos remembers sitting under the shade trees along the wrought iron fence that enclosed the church grounds and listening to the *viejos*, old men, who gathered there to smoke and tell stories on warm summer evenings. "That church," he says, "was the center of our neighborhood, the place where people came together," until Las Cruces discovered urban renewal.

Between 1968 and 1972, Las Cruces revived and rebuilt its antiquated downtown. *Revive* and *rebuild* in this case meant level the old and destroy the past. In the fever to modernize downtown, many of the historic adobes were torn down to make way for parking lots. Main Street was closed off to car traffic, replaced by a pedestrian mall. The charming old brick and adobe storefronts that survived the wrecking ball were "improved" by the addition of bland metal facades. Buildings that once housed bustling stores and restaurants are now quiet, occupied by low-rent tenants such as social service agencies and off-brand churches. An undistinguished modern post office replaces Carlos's uncle's crowded hardware store. The "racetrack," an oval-shaped thoroughfare that splits into one-way streets three lanes wide on each side of downtown, was built to speed traffic through the area. It does. People drive through now but rarely stop, hurrying somewhere else. Only on Farmer's Market mornings, twice a week, does downtown again fill with people. Far from reviving Las Cruces's downtown, urban renewal nearly killed it. As the years pass, fewer and fewer Las Crucens remember when the deserted pedestrian mall was a thriving town center.

Las Cruces's downtown might have survived its well-intentioned but thoughtless urban renewal but for one thing: the destruction of St. Genevieve's. Church Street still marks the boundary between the barrio and downtown, but it is not the Church Street that Carlos Sanchez and many others grew up with. A steel and glass bank building rises where the twin towers of St. Genevieve's used to be; a sea of asphalt parking lots replaces the churchyard that served as community center, recreation place, and informal town hall. No traces of Saint Genevieve's remain. The spreading shade trees where Carlos used to listen to the old ones gossip, talk, and tell their stories are long gone. When the wrecking balls destroyed Saint Genevieve's, they cut out the downtown's heart. The wound has not healed. The *viejos* and *viejas* have no gathering place now; today's kids, Carlos says sadly, listen to MTV instead.

Grizzly bears, Mogollon, Manso, St. Genevieve's . . . How much of our heritage have we wiped out in our arrogance, or simply forgotten? As a newcomer to this Chihuahuan Desert country, I am captured by the stories of the old ones. They tell of the way things used to be, reminding us of, as Joy Harjo says, "the possibility of everything you can't see." The old stories tell of grizzly bears hunting desert grasslands and wooded riverbank bosques. They tell of the viejos gathered around Saint Genevieve's, of the Tortugas, of their ancestors, the almost-forgotten Manso themselves descendants of the Mogollon who long ago chipped the grizzly bear footprint into the volcanic boulder atop the ridge at Three Rivers. These stories provide a rich heritage for all of us who live in this intractable Chihuahuan Desert country—newcomers, old-timers, Anglos, Latinos, and Native Americans alike.

Stories offer us more than a heritage. Stories can teach us how to live in this seemingly desolate landscape, how to take joy from the desert. We need stories if we are to have a future here, just as, after the long drought, the Mogollon needed the stories of their hunting and gathering ancestors, the Chihuahua Archaic, in order to survive, and just as the village of Tortugas has adapted the stories from their Pueblo and Mejicano heritage to root themselves in this landscape and survive in today's changing world.

Stories give us roots, linking us to this landscape; stories show us how to behave if we are to live on for generation after generation in this difficult and beautiful Chihuahuan Desert. Stories carry our culture without which we are lost. We must teach, pass on, listen to, and learn from the experience of those who came before us. We must not forget the stories.

Weeds

*"Weed—Any plant or vegetation,
. . . interfering with the objectives or
requirements of people."*
European Weed Research Society, statutes, article III, 1975

"No human being is illegal."
Eli Wiesel

On the afternoon of Wednesday, July 1, 1992, the Doña Ana County Sheriff's Office responded to the report of a body in the desert near War Road on the Texas–New Mexico border some thirty miles southeast of Las Cruces. Sheriff's officers arriving at the scene found the body of an older, dark-skinned Latino man, about 5 foot 2 inches tall with salt-and-pepper, shoulder-length hair. He was lying face down in the dirt near the signs marking the state boundary, just eighteen inches over the line in New Mexico. Despite the hundred-plus-degree heat of that summer afternoon, he was dressed in several layers of clothing: a blue sweater patterned with stylized birds and colorful stripes on top, another sweater under that, faded blue button-fly Levi's and a pair of gold corduroy jeans underneath, black socks, and black leather tennis shoes tied with baling wire.

He had been there a while. Employees driving War Road to work at White Sands Missile Range had first spotted the man nearby five days before on Friday, June 26. He was carrying a gallon jug of water, a white straw cowboy hat protecting his head from the merciless sun. According to one witness, he was last seen alive sitting on the ground, propped up against the state boundary signposts "looking sick," still wearing the cowboy hat, still carrying the plastic jug, on Monday, June 29. By Wednesday afternoon, he was dead, his sun-blackened body bloated and stinking, his discarded water jug empty. He had died of thirst.

War Road, so called because it links northeast El Paso with the sprawling army facilities of Fort Bliss and White Sands Missile Range, runs through the desolate creosote bush desert across the Franklin and Organ Mountains from my house in Las Cruces. It is the main route to and from work for hundreds of El Paso–area commuters bound for the Missile Range. Near where the man died is the main entrance to a cattle ranch. As they zipped by in their air-conditioned vehicles, passers-by could not have missed seeing the man as he stood just a few yards from the road, growing increasingly delirious from hunger and thirst. Yet only a handful of people responded to the pleas of the sheriff's office for witnesses who had seen or talked to the unidentified man. Several reported seeing him; one couple said that they'd seen another driver stop and motion to him as if to offer a ride. But, according to Investigator Ed Miranda of the Doña Ana County Sheriff's Office, not one of the hundreds who must have driven by ever admitted to stopping to talk to or help him. If anyone played good Samaritan, they didn't admit it.

Fear is a powerful barrier. The dead man was an illegal immigrant, a Mexican national who had crossed the border without papers to come north. Title 8, section 1324 of the U.S. Code makes it a felony to "willfully or knowingly . . . transport . . . conceal, harbor, or shield from detection . . . any alien." For years, federal law forbade giving a ride to a migrant who had crossed the border without papers but not to pay that same person to mow your yard, clean your house, pick your orchard, or weed your chile field. Then came the Immigration Reform and Control Act of 1986, Public Law 99-603, which added "employ" to the list of ways you cannot assist an undocumented immigrant. Today's legal code imposes stiff penalties for "aiding and abetting" illegal immigrants: up to three thousand dollars and five years in jail for each migrant that you give a ride to, allow to sleep in your basement, or pay to work. It is probably not illegal to give a drink of water to a dehydrated and delirious illegal immigrant, but the law is unclear. Better to pretend that you didn't see him. Better to not get involved, even to save his life. Even if some Good Samaritan had overcome her or his own fear and had stopped to offer the now-dead man a ride, he might not have accepted the offer, paralyzed by his own barrier of fear: fear of the Border Patrol, which would arrest him and send him back across *La Frontera*; fear of gang members, thugs, and others who beat up, rob, and generally prey on illegal immigrants; fear of the unknown in this strange country.

We treated the man by the side of War Road as a human weed. He was in the way, unwanted. *Webster's New Universal Unabridged Dictionary* defines *weed* as "any undesired, uncultivated plant that grows in profusion so as to crowd out a desired crop, disfigure a lawn, etc.," or "something useless." An agricultural definition calls a weed "any plant or vegetation, . . . interfering with the objectives or requirements of people." Clearly, a weed is something that we consider an obstacle. *Weed* is a subjective label, not a scientific truth. One person's weed is another's wildflower.

The definition of weed is also clearly flexible. Whether something is a weed or not depends on one's personal viewpoint; how we see things changes as conditions change, and varies over time. One thing remains constant: *Weed* is always derogatory. It designates "other," something or someone that we consider an obstacle to our own success. A weed is ineligible for compassion. A weed is less a reflection of our knowledge than of our prejudices and fears.

In 1894, E. O. Wooton, the first botanist at the New Mexico College of Agriculture and Mechanic Arts (now New Mexico State University) in Las Cruces, wrote a treatise on New Mexico's weeds. His "List of Several of the Worst Weeds of the Southern Part of the Territory with Notes on Each" details nineteen plants, all but one of which are native to the area. Time, new technology, and changing cultural values have radically changed the status of Wooton's worst weeds. Many are no longer problems; some are even valued for their beauty or utility. For example, the common sunflower or *mira sol*, described by Wooton as taking "complete possession of fence corners, roadsides, and ditches and . . . ever encroaching on the cultivated fields," is no longer so common. Herbicides have nearly eliminated it here in the Mesilla Valley. Indeed, a variety of the common sunflower has been completely absolved of weed status and is now grown as a profitable crop.

We treat some human beings like weeds. Just as we may decide that a particular plant is in our way, we sometimes deem whole groups of human beings in the way, threats to our livelihood, security, or prosperity. When we refused asylum to boatloads of Haitian refugees, and sent them home to slow starvation or death squads, we were treating them as weeds. When we seized Native American lands in trade for reservations much like the impoverished black "homelands" of South Africa, we treated them as weeds. When we allow our police forces to harass young blacks or Latinos just because of their skin color and dress, we are treating them as weeds.

The dead man's name was Ramón Vasquez Ramírez. After extensive inquiries in Mexico and the United States, Investigator Miranda finally learned his name from old fingerprint records maintained by the Federal Bureau of Investigation in Quantico, Virginia. Besides his name, the FBI record simply says that he was born in 1923, in Atotonilco, Jalisco, in the tropical highlands of México some fifteen hundred miles south of where he died. Beyond that, the records are silent. Nor did his body say much more. His pockets held neither identification nor family pictures. He died with just six dollars, a cigarette lighter, and a book of matches. With so few details, it is impossible to be certain of Vasquez Ramírez's story. But some things can be inferred. The style of his ivory-colored straw cowboy hat, stiffly creased with an upturned brim, suggests that he was a country-dweller. His short stature, dark mahogany skin, and the broad cheekbones of his face say that he was probably more Indian than Spanish. Bad teeth tell of a life of poverty with no dental care. His plastic water jug says that he was planning to travel through the desert.

Vasquez Ramírez died just outside of Chaparral, New Mexico, the outer edge of the El Paso–Juárez metropolitan area. How did he end up in the desert alongside War Road some twenty miles north of the border? Perhaps he had been dropped at the state line by a *coyote*, a smuggler, who, for a stiff fee in cash, transports human beings across the United States–Mexican border. Maybe the smuggler demanded more money than Vasquez Ramírez possessed and when he couldn't pay enough, the coyote abandoned him there. Or perhaps thugs robbed him and then dropped him off in the desert.

Maybe he was waiting for a ride further north, a ride that never came. Or perhaps, too poor to even afford a coyote, Vasquez Ramírez was headed north on foot, alone.

If so, he faced a perilous journey. Ahead of him lay a hundred miles of desert, blazing in the summer heat. Twenty-five miles north—a very long day's walk in hundred-degree temperatures—sprouts the small cluster of buildings that make up the headquarters of White Sands Missile Range. The next human habitation, some thirty-five miles across the open desert, is Holloman Air Force Base, and fifteen miles beyond it is Alamogordo, a military town not known for its friendliness to Mejicanos. Beyond Alamogordo stretches the desert offering neither shade to soften the scorching midday sun nor shelter from the bone-chilling night air, peopled by four-footed coyotes, by rattlesnakes and scorpions, studded by all manner of spiny plants and unexploded army weapons, and marked only by the army's gravel roads, barbed wire fences, tank tracks, and bomb craters. But to an illegal immigrant, the desert might seem safer than the occasional towns, where he is more likely to meet *La Migra*, the Border Patrol, or cholos.

If possible, most illegal immigrants bypass the desert entirely. Those with enough money buy counterfeit papers and travel north on a flight high above the desert on a commercial airplane. For the many who cannot afford plane fares, the next best and considerably cheaper way is to watch the desolate landscape roll by from an airconditioned bus. Those without papers may pay coyotes to smuggle them north. These people—called *pollos*, chickens, in México, a term indicating clearly the prey-predator relationship with those who smuggle them—make the journey like so many sacks of contraband, sometimes stuffed into suffocatingly small compartments in trunks, trailers, or under the floors of a coyote's vans, or even herded into empty cars on freight trains. The coyotes may not bother to figure out where the train is going. The pollos may die from suffocation or heat exhaustion if the train cars end up parked on a siding in the desert and the frightened occupants are unable to open the airtight doors, or may freeze if the train goes north into winter weather they are not prepared for. The poorest undocumented immigrants, unable to afford coyotes, may hitch their own rides on freight trains, risking heatstroke by clinging to car roofs, or decapitation by hooking themselves onto the framework underneath the cars, inches from the track rushing by. Or they may band together and hike across the desert in groups, moving at night. But to cross the desert alone, on foot, is rare. A very poor, very desperate person might attempt it in order to find a job and secure for himself a slice of the good life in *El Norte* or in order to join a family already safely merged into the Latino neighborhoods of Albuquerque, Denver, Los Angeles, or Chicago.

Vasquez Ramírez's swollen and sun-blackened body cannot tell us where he was headed and what happened. It says only that he had probably crossed the border before at least once; his fingerprints in that old FBI file date to an arrest in 1951, most likely for illegal entry into the United States. But this last time, Ramón Vasquez Ramírez was not successful. Instead of finding a job and his small piece of prosperity, he died a slow, horrible death.

Investigator Miranda's photographs bear mute witness to Vasquez Ramírez' lonely agony: His plastic water jug, a gallon size that once held Price's Lowfat Milk, lies empty and abandoned on the dusty ground across the road from his body. A cluster of round, green, softball-sized wild buffalo gourds, the kind called *chichicoyotas*, trickster breasts, in México for their stomach-wrenching bitterness, lie nearby, their green surfaces scoured by human teeth marks, like the frantic nibbling of a starving mouse. (Despite the gourds's succulent appearance, few desert animals eat buffalo gourd. The poisons that cause their bitter taste produce nausea, cramps, and vomiting or diarrhea in humans.) Another photo shows only a blackened stain on the ground, the remains of a bloody pool of vomit or diarrhea perhaps caused by the buffalo gourd that Vasquez Ramírez nibbled in desperate thirst. Other photos show scuff marks in the dry, tan soil around his body; his empty right shoe lies kicked away from his black-stockinged right foot, a record of a man thrashing around in delirium before succumbing to the merciful oblivion of unconsciousness. The death of Ramón Vasquez Ramírez, in full view of a well-traveled road, is not a pretty story.

❧

In the late 1870s, Ukrainian farmers in Bon Homme County, South Dakota, inadvertently sowed the seeds of the West's worst weed epidemic when they broke the tough prairie sod to plant flax seed brought from their homes in Russia's arid shrub steppes. Unbeknownst to the farmers, another Russian immigrant, tumbleweed, had hitchhiked a ride along with the flax. Within less than two decades, aided by the wholesale plowing of the prairies, tumbleweed had bounced its way across the Great Plains and was sprouting throughout the West.

The spiny weed, also called Russian thistle, popped up quickly wherever the soil was bare, crowding out crops in fields, clogging irrigation ditches, and spoiling pastures. Its strong spines tore at the flesh of threshing crews and their horses; its seeds fouled grain harvests. Highly flammable, tumbleweed spread prairie fires by rolling and leaping across fire lines to set houses and crops ablaze. Panic-stricken farmers in some places began abandoning their farms.

Drastic eradication measures were proposed. Edward T. Kearney, a North Dakota legislator, imagined building a wire fence around his state to keep tumbleweed out. The Wisconsin Experiment Station suggested that a tumbleweed plant be placed in every schoolhouse and the children be taught to kill it "as they would a rattlesnake." New Mexico's E.O. Wooton urged: "Kill it all and now. . . . Never let a single plant bear seed."

Eradication proved impossible. Given a home by poor farming and ranching practices and transport by railroads and irrigation ditches, tumbleweed, the weed that the Hopi call "white man's plant," spread like wildfire across disturbed ground in the West. By the time the Sons of the Pioneers recorded their hit song "Tumbling Tumbleweeds" in 1934, this invader had become such an integral part of its adopted land that it symbolized the West.

There is a heart-wrenching irony here. Tumbleweed, a plant that has come to stand for the West in popular American culture, is truly alien. But the human "weeds" migrating north from Mexico and Latin America belong here. Descended in part from the Maya, Quecha, Aztec, and other ancient cultures of Latin America, these people have more claim to the term *native* than pale-skinned *norteñas* like me. My roots in this American soil are not nearly as deep. My grandfather, my father's father, Olav Tweit, emigrated from Norway in 1917; his wife, my grandmother Christine Farquharson, was the youngest daughter of a Scottish immigrant. Although my mother's family traces some of its roots in America back to the 1700s, most of her Swedish and English forbearers are much more recent arrivals. Yet our political system gives me a citizenship right denied Vasquez Ramírez and his kind; no matter that the cultural right, the right of long-term tenancy, of roots in this American landscape, is clearly theirs. If anyone is an "alien" here, it is newcomers like me.

Even supposing that we could—or should—draw the line between who belongs here and who doesn't, it is no more possible to stop the tide of illegal immigrants like Ramón Vasquez Ramírez than it was to stop the spread of tumbleweed. Between three hundred thousand and half-a-million people enter the United States illegally each year according to a 1993 report by the federal Commission on Agricultural Workers. The number of illegal immigrants in this country is tough to figure, since people afraid of being deported are understandably reluctant to fill out questionnaires. Still, experts estimate that at least 3.5 million such "undocumented" people live amongst us. Some eighty-five to ninety percent of them, like Vasquez Ramírez, come from México.

The United States's border with México stretches two thousand miles from the Gulf of Mexico to the Pacific Ocean. Beginning at Brownsville, Texas–Matamoros, Mexico on the Gulf Coast, it runs up the Río Grande River for twelve hundred miles to where the river turns north into New Mexico. There the border cuts west across the arid grasslands and deserts of southern New Mexico, Arizona, and southern California. It ends where the southern California chaparral meets the Pacific Ocean between San Diego, California, and Tijuana, México. Most of this immense sweep of landscape is "unpopulated," that is, home to many times more jack-rabbits and harvester ants than people. Tiny towns like Antelope Wells, New Mexico, too small to be noted by my Rand–McNally Road Atlas, home to just a handful of people and a border station, dot the lonely miles.

The United States' side of this immense stretch of landscape is patrolled by some thirty-five hundred agents of the Border Patrol (the agency will not reveal the exact number), the police agency of the Immigration and Naturalization Service. These one-and-a-half agents per linear border mile are assisted by local police, state police and county sheriff's officers. The humans of the Border Patrol depend on billions of dollars of advanced technology: electronic ground sensors that detect and report the motion of passing humans to monitors at border patrol stations, land-based and airborne infrared imaging equipment, low-light-level television systems on posts along frequently traveled sections of the border, and helicopters equipped with "Nite Sun" searchlights and infrared radar with heat-sensing capabilities. Still, at its own estimate, the Border Patrol intercepts only one of every three people who enter the country illegally each year. We are asking them to do an impossible job.

The numbers are on the migrants's side. The 625 Border Patrol agents based in the El Paso sector are responsible for patrolling 289 miles of the international boundary, plus 125,000 square miles of landscape—the whole of New Mexico and that portion of west Texas including El Paso. In fiscal year 1992, they picked up 252,066 deportable immigrants, an average of 600 to 900 people per *day*, most of those along the border between El Paso and Juárez, where illegal migrants can simply dash across the political line and blend into crowds of resident Latinos on the United States's side. Ninety-eight percent of the migrants caught by the Border Patrol come from México. Since most Mexican immigrants without papers are simply deported voluntarily—unless they have a criminal record—it is impossible to tell how many of these arrests represent repeaters. Sometimes a deportee will be picked up crossing the border again within an hour after processing.

On a tour of the El Paso–Juárez-area border with Doug Mosier, public affairs officer with the Border Patrol's El Paso sector, I watched dozens of people cross the narrow, concrete-lined waterway of the Río Grande, going from Juárez to El Paso—from legal to illegal, from native to weed—by simply crossing a muddy river. These commuters bypassed official entrance stations on the bridges by riding the informal system of commuter "ferries" across the river itself. Most were simple affairs: a truck tire inner tube with a piece of plywood serving as a deck, towed across by a ferryman who wades or swims depending on the depth of the river. Men and women, some holding a child tightly by the arm, lined up on the Juárez bank of the river waiting for each ferry. Just across the river from the Border Patrol processing station in downtown El Paso itself was an actual ferry boat, a small aluminum skiff bearing the neatly painted name *Río Bravo Trabajo Social*, "Río Grande Social Work." Its mustachioed captain did a brisk trade carrying customers across the river. Those too poor to afford ferry fare simply undressed and waded or swam across, holding their clothes out of the water. (Wet clothes mark one as distinctly déclassé in El Paso.) It was all part of the morning commute.

Once across the river, the commuters scrambled up the

cement embankment on the United States side and collected in small groups just outside of holes torn in the eight-foot-high chain link fence, waiting until no pale green Border Patrol vans were in sight. When the coast was clear, they would dash across the levy road and cross an adjacent railroad yard, and disappear in downtown El Paso. Border Patrol policy, said Doug Mosier, forbids arresting migrants near the river because of the danger of drownings. Patrol agents therefore wait until the illegal immigrants are away from the river before attempting to nab them.

Since I toured the border, the patrol has begun "Operation Hold-the-Line," stationing 400 of its agents within sight of each other in a twenty-four-hour watch along a twenty-mile-long stretch of the Juárez–El Paso border. Operation Hold-the-Line has slowed the flow of illegal crossers in that area to a trickle: apprehensions of undocumented immigrants are down to around two hundred per day. But the police line is horrifically expensive, costing U.S. taxpayers $250,000 in overtime for its first two weeks alone, and has also strained relations between the two cities. Further, it seems to have only deflected the flow, other border towns are reporting up to two hundred percent increases in illegal crossings. More people are crossing the desert, and more are dying as they try. Crime in El Paso is down some, according to a recent study by professors at University of Texas at El Paso but, by concentrating agents on the border, Operation Hold-the-Line has made it easier for those who do make it across to work illegally in El Paso. Once border-crossers are in El Paso, they need not fear La Migra will pick them up.

As we drove along in the air-conditioned Border Patrol sedan, isolated behind tinted windows, I felt profoundly uneasy. I do not visit La Frontera often; I have traveled to Juárez only twice since we moved here. The discontinuity of the Border—relative wealth on one side of La Frontera, poverty on the other—rubs my conscience raw. The ugly, eight-foot-high chain link fences and uniformed police patrolling this artificial line make the boundary between peoples seem as cruel as the now-torn-down Berlin Wall. Besides good fortune—largely a matter of luck—and pale skin, what separates me from the neatly dressed people who cross the river to work in El Paso each day? Not much. I wanted to get out and talk to the groups of people on the other side of the fence, but I did not know what to say. Instead, I took the coward's way out and waved at the people that we passed, feeling very much like the rich American. To my surprise, since I was riding in a Migra patrol car, many smiled and waved back.

ॐ

When the Ukrainian farmers of Bon Homme County, South Dakota, stripped the thick prairie sod from atop the black soil to plant their crops, they had no idea that, once they bared the soil, devastating weed infestations were inevitable. Before they plowed the prairies, the dense thatch of grasses left no space for weed seeds to germinate. But once thousands of acres of rich soil were bare, nothing prevented weeds from taking over this new, fertile habitat. Tumbleweed's lickety-split spread across the West was made possible by the farming practices of the day.

So, too, with humans. Today's human migrants are drawn by opportunity, by the promise of jobs, the chance to earn money and live a comfortable life very different from that of the impoverished and crowded conditions of their home places. Per-family income in Latin America averages around twenty-three hundred dollars per year; in the United States, per-family income averages nearly ten times that, or over twenty thousand per year. Unemployment rates are stuck at around forty percent in México, nearly one of every two people cannot find work. In rural México and the Central American–refugee-clogged south, unemployment rises to eighty or even ninety percent. Just as the plowing of the prairies gave tumbleweed and other adventitious plants the opportunity to spread, so, too, does the promise of economic opportunity, real or not, lure today's human migrants north. We all seek an environment where we can flourish. If to find that, we must cross La Frontera despite the laws and risks, so be it. Dreams and aspirations are powerful motivators.

103

No one knows how many who cross the border surreptitiously survive the trip. Ramón Vasquez Ramírez's fate is not uncommon, except for the public aspect. From the hoods who hang out on the United States bank of the Río Grande and extort money or sexual favors from those who swim, wade, or ride across, to the gangs and *banditos* on the Mexican side who congregate near popular border crossing spots to rob, rape, and sometimes kill helpless migrants, to the coyotes who rob their pollos before abandoning them, the border is a dangerous place. Accurate statistics are hard to come by, since illegal immigrants are understandably reluctant to report crimes to the police, who might deport them. But the scattering of information available is sobering. Between 1984 and 1989, fifteen hundred people are known to have died along the busiest section of the line, the California–México border. In 1989 alone, 117 bodies of drowning victims were recovered just from the Lower Río Grande Valley in south Texas. Fifty-three of those were never identified, and no one knows how many more bodies were never found. The total in 1992 was closer to two hundred; bodies are so commonly pulled from the river now that some authorities refer to the dead people casually as "floaters." A year spent reading border newspapers is enlightening, and numbing. Stories of accidents to border crossers are routine. Besides the floaters, people die or are injured when trying to board or leave moving freight trains; they are raped, beaten, and shot by thieves, gangs, or American hate groups; they suffocate in coyotes's vans, trailers or in locked train cars; they are hit and killed while trying to run across highways; or, like Ramón Vasquez Ramírez, they die of exposure in the inhospitable desert.

Then there is official violence. In México, immigrants must slip past the national and local police without being caught or be subject to beatings, torture, and extortion of money and/or sexual favors. (At the 1989 meeting of the Border Commission on Human Rights, Mexican participants reported 826 "disappeared" persons along the border in México.) In 1992, then-Mexican president Carlos Salinas de Gortari raised the salaries of federal police and border inspectors, vowing to root out corruption. So far, the effect on the largely poor, powerless, and uneducated migrants is not clear. Mexican officials are reluctant to discuss migrants; their continuing flight across the border is an embarrassment to that country.

Nor is this side of the border the promised land. Once safely inside the United States, immigrants like Ramón Vasquez Ramírez often face discrimination, harassment, and worse. Roberto Martínez of the Immigration Law Enforcement Monitoring Project in San Diego keeps tabs on La Migra and other immigration law enforcement agencies in the United States. A recent report from his group, covering the two years from May of 1989 to May of 1991, tallies 1,273 instances of abuses ranging from sexual and physical abuse, including seven deaths, to denial of due process. The deaths are especially poignant, a record of extreme frustration or hatred erupting into violence. For example, seventeen-year-old Ismael Ramírez died of a brain hemorrhage after a Border Patrol agent lifted him up and threw him down on the street while questioning him in Madera, California. Attorneys for Ramírez's family say this was at least the fifth incident of serious misconduct in the agent's career; the others included a death by vehicle run-down and the beatings of legal immigrants. Eleven months later, the agent was promoted. In another case, a Border Patrol van ran down and killed Luis Eduardo Hernandez as he was trying to slip back through the border fence into México. His family sued the Border Patrol and was awarded fifty-thousand dollars in damages.

I asked Roberto Martínez if the violence had abated since the 1991 report. "Yes, and no," he said. There had been just one killing in the most recent two-year period, he explained, perhaps because of the publicity brought on by the Immigration Law Enforcement Monitoring Project. But physical and sexual abuse, he thought, were on the rise. Just the previous week, Martínez said, he had taken half a dozen victims of physical abuse that week alone to hearings. One twenty-year-old Mexican national was kicked so badly by Border Patrol agents that he nearly died from injuries to his pancreas. Martínez told of a Border Patrol agent recently sentenced to prison for kidnapping and raping a sixteen-year-old Mexican girl from a migrant labor camp in the United States. After raping her, Martínez said, the agent deported the girl to keep her from testifying against him.

Beatings and harassment are not confined to illegal immigrants; all Latinos, legal residents and citizens alike, and people who look Latino are subject to abuse. In El Paso, students and faculty of Bowie High School, a predominantly Latino high school in a neighborhood next to the border, filed a class action lawsuit against the Border Patrol for continuing harassment. They allege that Border Patrol agents routinely swept the school grounds, picking up all present and taking them to the border for questioning on the presumption that they look like illegal immigrants. On July 15, 1989, Border Patrol agents picked up Pedro Garcia, a nineteen-year-old Bowie High School student and a legal resident, handcuffed him, and drove him to the Paso del Norte Bridge (the border station) to question him because he was not carrying his Green Card, proof of legal residency. "Questioning" in this case involved banging his face against the wall and kicking him.

The Border Patrol dismisses these cases as rarities, problems with "a few bad apples," inevitable in trying to do an impossible job. In El Paso, faced with the Bowie High School suit and other lawsuits, the Border Patrol has begun a pilot sensitivity training project for its agents, has recently set up a twenty-four-hour phone line to receive complaints and comments, and has established a community relations board.

Even if immigrants to El Norte manage to successfully settle and find work, they still face extreme prejudice. Like Ramón Vasquez Ramírez, many are the poorest of the rural poor, with little or no formal education. Many Latinos (and non-Latinos) in the United States despise these *paisanos* as the underclass. Segregated by their lack of English, their lack of education, and their low social status, they keep to their own

Spanish-speaking communities. Although they may be highly skilled, their skills as storytellers, curanderos, carvers, weavers, potters, and small farmers do not count for much in our society. I was surprised to discover how rigid is the social stratification, how bitter the prejudice against *mojados*, wetbacks, the derisive term for newly arrived illegals.

Take my friend Cruz and her husband Adrian. Cruz, one of eleven brothers and sisters, was sent north from Guadalajara by her family about four years ago. Determined to finish her education—her dream is to graduate from beauty school and become a hairdresser—she lied about her age in order to enroll in junior high school. After graduating, she married Adrian, born in Torreón, Chihuahua, but now a resident of the United States. They both work hard to make ends meet. Adrian cleans a store at night and bags groceries by day; Cruz struggles to learn English and finish her G.E.D., cleans houses, does ironing, and looks after their two children. It is Cruz's determination that pushes their family towards a better life. Adrian became a United States's citizen at her urging; recently, she parlayed their income tax refund into the down payment on a tiny piece of land for their house trailer. Ironically, Adrian's family, immigrants who arrived here just fifteen years before Cruz, treats Cruz like dirt. Some days she despairs. If she could, Cruz says, she would return home to Guadalajara and her family. But there is no work there, economics keeps Cruz here in the strange, hard world of the United States. It is a bitter necessity. "Here," she said to me one day, fierce pride mixing with tears, "I am a nobody, just a *mojada*."

Despite all, people continue to come north. As I wrote this essay, twenty-nine-year-old Oscar Cardenas said goodbye to his wife and children in Palomas, México, a border town in northern Chihuahua about sixty miles southwest of Las Cruces, and set out on foot across the desert with his twenty-year-old cousin Chumel Cardenas Castillo, and his cousin's friend Lalo. They intended to walk to a ranch near Albuquerque, New Mexico, some two-hundred-fifty miles north, to work. A day later, while crossing a ranch outside the town of Deming, New Mexico, about thirty miles north of Palomas, they ran out of water and became separated. Chumel Cardenas Castillo and his friend turned around and headed home. Oscar Cardenas, chased by wild animals—probably peccaries, boarlike creatures with sharp tusks—fell out of a tree and broke his leg. He crawled to a nearby cattle watering tank and lay there for five days without food, drinking the water from the cattle tank. Cardenas was lucky. The ranch owners found him, close to death, and took him to the hospital. Oscar Cardenas recovered and was sent home to Palomas two weeks after he and his cousin and friend left to walk north. Later that summer, the desert claimed the lives of a Salvadoran woman and a Guatemalan man.

When E. O. Wooton, the botanist at the New Mexico College of Agriculture in Las Cruces, wrote his treatise on New Mexico's weeds in 1894, it was a group of natives, including globemallow, blueweed, and common sunflower, that he considered most vexing. Wooton could not have imagined how time would change his list of worst weeds. As farming practices changed, especially with the chemical herbicides developed after World War II, the perennial natives that Wooton worried about became less and less troublesome. Most are no longer considered problems today. Some, like globemallow, have changed status completely and are now valued as wildflowers; others, like common sunflower, are grown as crops. Wooton's 1894 list didn't mention tumbleweed, that opportunistic alien. Yet within a decade, tumbleweed had swept across the region, taking over cultivated fields, overgrazed rangelands, abandoned farms, and other disturbed ground all across the West. It and other annuals, most introduced, are today's "worst weeds." Tumbleweed not only flourishes still, but this introduced foreigner is so firmly rooted here that it has come to symbolize the West in popular culture.

When does a weed become a problem, something that we root out, spray with herbicides, destroy? Why do we tolerate or ignore some people and then suddenly focus our fear and hatred on them? A few tumbleweeds were no cause for panic. It was only when the invader spread like fire across the bared soils of the West that farmers, legislators, and others began calling for drastic measures to halt the "scourge of the West." When weeds multiply, we see them as a threat to our existence. But it is not that simple. Sometimes weeds are the fall guy, taking the rap for conditions caused by a complicated array of problems.

At the time that grain farmers of the northern Great Plains were panicking and abandoning their tumbleweed-infested farms in the 1890s, a national financial panic was causing widespread farm and bank failures. Easier to blame the foreigners, like invading tumbleweed, than to confront the more complex reality of economics, politics, and culture. These days are similarly uneasy times: The number of low-skill, high-paying industrial jobs continues to decline. In the past decade, major corporations have laid off hundreds of thousands of employees. A college degree no longer guarantees a job. We are frightened for our futures. Rather than tackling the difficult issues involved in today's conditions, we look for a simple solution—someone to blame. Someone who is not "us." "Aha!" we say when we see the hundreds, or thousands, of Vasquez Ramírezes crossing the border. It is "their" fault. "They" are taking our jobs, swelling the welfare rolls, filling our schools with Spanish-speakers, draining our state and federal treasuries dry. So we slam the gates shut, circle the wagons, put up the "No Vacancy" signs.

110　　In 1989, we cheered as the Berlin Wall came down. Half a decade later, we are building our own Berlin Wall along the United States–Mexican border. Between San Diego and Tijuana, the most-heavily traveled section of La Frontera, a wall of ten-foot-tall steel planks now replaces the chain link fence. ("The Tortilla Curtain Goes Steel," reported one newspaper headline.) Steel walls are scheduled to go up along other sections of the border, including one just south of where I live, between Sunland Park, New Mexico, and Colonia Anapra, a squatters's suburb of Ciudad Juárez. Edward T. Kearney, the North Dakota legislator who proposed building a wire fence around his state to keep tumbleweed out, would be proud. California, the state that is home to the most illegal immigrants, recently passed Proposition 187, a law that would bar resident illegal immigrants and their children— even if legal residents—from receiving any government services, including public education, all but emergency medical care, and welfare or disaster assistance. The message is loud and clear: "We don't want you. Go home."

In fact, whose "home" is this? We Americans are newcomers, having wrested this northern Chihuahuan Desert country from Vasquez Ramírez' country in the Mexican-American War between 1846 and 1848. The current United States–México border is a political line imposed across a people, artificially dividing the residents into "Mexicans" and "Americans." Many still have family on both sides of the line, another echo of the Berlin Wall. Who, then, are the "natives" and who are the "weeds"?

In the early 1800s, before the United States acquired by force, by purchase, and by treaty what is now the Southwest, a stream of American citizens were already encroaching illegally onto this foreign territory, looking for profits to be made trading, trapping, mining, and farming. During that period, the fledgling government of México, worried about securing what is now Texas against the French, invited Americans to apply for land and, if accepted, colonize the area and become Mexican citizens. Many did. But others avoided the official process and moved in on their own as "illegal aliens." The private land agents set up to process American settlers complained bitterly about the illegals, whom they considered to be "wanderers" and "ne'er-do-wells" harmful to the well-being of the territory. Sound familiar?

Many Mejicanos are newcomers too, descendants of the Spaniards who wrenched this Chihuahuan Desert country from the resident Native Americans in the 1500s and 1600s. Even Native Americans came from somewhere else: the Apaches, Athapaskan speakers most closely related to Aleuts, moved down from the North as recently as the 1400s, encroaching on the resident Manso, Jano, Suma, Jumano, Piro, and Tewa peoples. These cultures, descendants of the Mogollon and Anasazi, are themselves descended from "illegal aliens," migrants who probably arrived in what is now the

Chihuahuan Desert from the steppes of Siberia as recently as fifteen thousand years ago. The history of "illegal immigration" to the Southwest is thus a long one.

Immigrants from México were not always seen as weeds. When the United States first began to restrict immigration in the late 1800s, Americans were not concerned about migrants from south of the border at all. The first exclusion acts aimed to stop the flow of people from across the Pacific. In the Go-West-Young-Man boom days after the Civil War, thousands of Chinese, mostly from Kwangtung Province around Canton, came east to the West as contract laborers. They built our railroads, dug our mines, and tilled our farm fields. In his book *Border*, a history of the United States–México boundary, historian Leon Metz calls the Chinese the "economic precursors to the Mexicans." Willing to work cheaply in conditions intolerable to others, many Chinese came, stayed long enough to satisfy their contract and accumulate what in China was a fortune, and returned home.

As the West's boom years were punctured by economic hard times, public feeling turned against the Chinese. Trade unions and newspaper editorials excoriated the "yellow peril" for taking jobs from American laborers. Fueled by the growing climate of hatred, mobs of toughs beat up or lynched anyone who looked Oriental, looted their stores and restaurants, and burned Chinese neighborhoods. But just as immigrants continue to come to El Norte today, neither violence nor prejudice nor laws stemmed the flow of Chinese. Plenty of Chinese needed the work; plenty of American employers wanted cheap, hard-working laborers. After Canada banned their passage, the Chinese slipped across the border from México. Coyotes of the day guided them across the border to Chinatowns in western cities, a situation eerily similar to today's Latino migrants.

In those years, Mexicans were welcome. They took the place of the now-banned Chinese in railroad construction and in working the huge areas of agricultural land created by new federal water projects in the Southwest. In fact, when Congress appropriated 1 million dollars in 1924 to create the Border Patrol, its mission was to prevent illegal European and Chinese immigration along the Mexican border, not to stop Mejicanos.

Then came the crash of 1929 and the Great Depression. Suddenly Mexican laborers were in the way; they were seen as taking American jobs: weeds. In an echo of the "yellow peril" of the late 1800s, prejudice against Mexicans and Mexican-Americans rose dramatically. People looking or sounding Mejicano were the target of harassment and violence. Between November 1929 and the end of 1931, over 350,000 Mexican nationals—and some Mexican Americans—left the United States for México, most voluntarily, taking advantage of free transportation, food for the journey, and even cash inducements offered by government agencies.

Not until World War II were Mexicans welcome across the border again, and then only under certain conditions. The Armed Forces, wartime industry, and internment camps absorbed the low-wage labor force, leaving western farmers literally helpless. Hence the "Bracero" agreement, a regulated program of contract labor that allowed American farmers (and railroads) during the war to import Mexican workers. As long as they came under the Bracero Program, Mexicans were welcome again.

In 1964, the door slammed shut again when the Bracero

Program was terminated. Nowadays, unless they are family members of permanent residents or of U. S. citizens, ordinary Mexicans like Oscar Cardenas or Ramón Vasquez Ramírez, have almost no chance to come here legally. We do not want them. They are weeds.

When my grandfather Olav came to the United States as an immigrant in 1917, he was seeking just what the migrants from México and Central America seek today: economic opportunity. He worked his way across the ocean from Norway doing hard, dangerous, low-paying work, shoveling coal into the blazing fires of ship's engines. The car factories of Detroit attracted this farm boy; he dreamed of becoming a design engineer. With just a high school education and no English, Olav started at the bottom, guiding freshly painted wooden wheel rims off of the assembly line at the Maxwell auto plant for thirty-one cents a day. By the time he married my grandmother Chris, the youngest daughter of a Scottish immigrant, he had learned English and had moved up to draftsman. Eventually, he achieved his dream and designed coke ovens for steel plants. But in 1917, newly arrived from impoverished Hardanger Fjord in rural Norway, what was then the "Third World," my grandfather Olav was surely just as much a weed as those who cross the border today. How many among us are the children and grandchildren of just such immigrants?

It seems to me that the only sin of immigrants like Oscar Cardenas and Ramón Vasquez Ramírez—or my grandfather Olav—is poverty. And poverty is no sin—it is something that we relatively well-off Americans fear. If we let too many of "them" in, "they" will take "our" jobs, bankrupt "our" schools, hospitals, and welfare systems; we will all be poor.

Indeed. The greatest and only poverty that we need fear is the spiritual and moral poverty resulting from our own lack of generosity.

We cannot draw arbitrary political lines in the desert and declare that one side is "ours" and the other "theirs." Such boundaries are imaginary. Poverty and crime cross them every day. So do air and water pollution, disease, and prejudice and fear. "They" are, in reality, "us." None of us—Anglos, Latinos, Native Americans—have a superior claim to belong here. In one way or another, we are all weeds. Our challenge is not to draw lines but to erase them. If we see immigrants like Cardenas and Ramírez as weeds, perhaps it is our vision that is at fault. As Ralph Waldo Emerson said, "A weed is a plant whose virtues have not yet been discovered."

What haunts me about Ramón Vasquez Ramírez is that we, who have plenty to share, allowed him to die. No, worse— we *watched* him die a horrible, prolonged death in the desert. If I had been speeding along War Road in my air-conditioned car to work at White Sands, would I have stopped? Would I have gone out of my way to help this slight, brown-skinned man? I wish that I could answer with an unswerving "yes." But I am not sure. It all depends, doesn't it, on whether we see the human being through our prejudices and fears. Would I see only his dirty sweater, his stained jeans, his bad teeth, and his obvious poverty and illegal status? Or would I see someone's well-loved brother, uncle, father, *abuelo*?

Investigator Ed Miranda of the Doña Ana County Sheriff's Office reports that, although he informed Mexican authorities about Ramón Vasquez Ramírez's death as soon as he identified Ramírez, no one ever claimed the body. In the end, Ramírez was given an indigent's burial by Crestview Mortuary in Albuquerque. Next time I go to Albuquerque, I think I'll visit him and put flowers on his grave.

Weeds. Who are they anyway?

Sanctuary

*All landscapes have a history. . . . There are distinct voices,
languages that belong to particular areas. There are voices
inside rocks, shallow washes, shifting skies; they are not silent.*
Joy Harjo, *Secrets from the Center of the World*

This is a sacred place, please behave accordingly.
Sign in the Cathedral of Saint Francis, Santa Fe
In Memory of Elsie Johnson *(1915–1994)*

On the first of April in 1918, Robert Lewis Cabe
boarded a train in tiny Hampton, Arkansas, bound for
Crossett to see a doctor at Crossett Hospital. Reverend Cabe,
a circuit-riding Methodist preacher, had been ill for months.
His parishioners, concerned about his deteriorating health,
had convinced him to see a doctor and had taken up a collection to pay for a two-month recuperative vacation.

After what Reverend Cabe's journal describes as "a most
extremely thorough examination," Dr. J. E. Sparks of Crossett
Hospital delivered the verdict: "Tuberculosis in a very active
form." His advice: "Go West at once if you expect to live."
The doctor recommended New Mexico. Although the elegant
script in Reverend Cabe's journal does not reveal his feelings, the diagnosis—essentially a death sentence—must have
stunned him. He was in his thirties and his life was going
well; he loved his work. He and his wife, Sarah Della Hope,
who was then six months pregnant, had five young children
and a comfortable house with a big garden and a cow.

Reverend Cabe took the 5:30 A.M. train home to Hampton the following day. Two weeks later, at noon on Thursday, April 18, having sold their house and most of their belongings, the family boarded a train "in a great downpour of rain," on their way to the desert Southwest. The following night, my husband's grandfather and his family reached El Paso, Texas, in the Chihuahuan Desert where Texas, New Mexico, and Old México meet. There they stopped.

The remaining daily notations in Reverend Cabe's journal, written in a sprawling and feeble hand, are brief and poignant. Saturday, April 20: "Ill day at the Hotel." Monday, April 22: "Too ill to write, but hunted for a house." The following Sunday, his terse note reflects his depression at having no spiritual flock to tend for the first time in many years: "A lonesome Sunday." Monday's entry is no better: "Nothing worthy of note." The diary ends two days later on Wednesday, May 1, with these words in a barely legible hand: "For the past month I have been so ill that nothing was of interest to me. I hope this month to be better." Reverend Cabe's hopes did not come true. He died of tuberculosis in El Paso three months later on August 13, 1918, leaving Sarah Della Hope on her own with seven children, including two-month-old twin boys, one of whom is now my father-in-law.

Until Richard was offered a teaching job in Las Cruces, we had paid little attention to Cabe family history. We did know that Richard's grandfather was buried in El Paso, Texas, just forty miles south of our new home, but we didn't know why. On a visit to Arkansas before we moved, Richard questioned his parents: Why was his grandfather buried in El Paso when his father had grown up in Arkansas? How long had the family lived in the Chihuahuan Desert? What had taken them there, so far from home? (Sarah Della Hope packed up the children and their belongings and took the train home after Reverend Cabe's death, and there they stayed. Arkansas remains home for this branch of the Cabe family.) In answer, Richard's mother dug out Reverend Cabe's diaries. Richard stayed up long after bedtime turning the pages of the cloth-bound ledgers, reading the faded handwriting: lists of sermons prepared and the dates they were used, columns of expenses, and page after page, book after book, of daily entries in neat handwriting on thin blue lines—the details of the life of a circuit-riding Methodist preacher. I was fast asleep long before he read the last few pages with their poignant story of Reverend Cabe's diagnosis and the family's desperate flight to the desert Southwest. I woke when Richard crawled into bed next to me, his face wet with tears. I held him close as he told me the story of the grandfather that he never knew, the man who died when Richard's own father was just an infant.

After we moved to Las Cruces, I read Reverend Cabe's journals again. Reading of the Cabe family's journey made our own difficult move to the desert seem infinitely easier. It put my acute feelings of dislocation and discomfort in perspective. Imagine how it felt, I thought, for these Arkansas natives, used to trees and rain and green, to be plunked down in this endlessly tan desert landscape. How in their dry-as-dust yard could they plant the huge garden that had fed them in Arkansas? Did Sarah Della Hope miss her flowers? Imagine them learning to cope with the musical cadences of Spanish instead of familiar Arkansas accents, with a culture as much Mexican as American. Imagine Sarah's feelings of despair as she gave birth to twin boys and cared for her ailing husband and their other five children while Reverend Cabe, her partner as well as her means of financial support, sank closer to death. The fact of their journey and their months in El Paso made our own move easier. Richard's family left footprints for us to follow. Reverend Cabe's grave down the valley gives us roots here— tenuous roots, but roots all the same—making this foreign landscape seem more like home.

When Richard first read his grandfather's journals, we wondered at the odd coincidence that sent the Cabe family to the same part of the Chihuahuan Desert where we settled seventy years later. Actually, their story was a common one. Reverend Cabe and his family, like hundreds of thousands of people suffering from tuberculosis, came to the Southwest in search of a health sanctuary in the hope that the dry air and mild climate would perform miracles that medicine of the day could not deliver.

For generations born after antibiotics revolutionized medicine, it is hard to imagine the magnitude and effect of tuberculosis. Dubbed the "White Plague" for its virulence (in contrast to the Black Plague of the Middle Ages), tuberculosis was the leading cause of death in nineteenth century America. By 1890, tuberculosis killed 150,000 Americans each year: or about 1.5 people out of every thousand. (By comparison, AIDS in 1990 killed nearly one per ten thousand.) Medical historians estimate that for every death, there were ten to twenty others seriously affected by the disease. At its height, tuberculosis claimed one-third of all Americans who died between the ages of fifteen and forty-four.

Tuberculosis is caused by a tiny, airborne bacteria, a parasite on human cells. As the bacteria grow and reproduce, they burst the walls of their host cells, forming lesions. In the most prevalent form of tuberculosis, the bacteria infect cells of the lung linings, causing the lungs to fill slowly with fluid. Soon the sufferer is literally gasping for breath, her or his lungs barely able to absorb oxygen. The common name of tuberculosis, "consumption," reflects the result: Without oxygen, food cannot be metabolized and the victim simply wastes away; flesh is seemingly "consumed" by the disease. Until the discovery and widespread use of antibiotics in the middle of the twentieth century, there was no cure. Some consumptives recovered. But in many cases, a diagnosis of tuberculosis condemned the sufferer to a slow, lingering death.

When Richard's grandfather was diagnosed with tuberculosis, the most promising treatment was just what Dr. Sparks of southern Arkansas's Crossett Hospital prescribed: Go West at once. Altitude Therapy, as this regimen was called, relied on the thinner air at elevations several thousand feet or more above sea level to give sufferers' afflicted lungs a rest, and on arid climates to dry out the tubercular lesions. The healthy air, reasoned adherents, would allow sufferers's lungs to heal. Fresh air was considered crucial. Patients spent hours at a time outside in all seasons, often lying on chaise lounges—hence the popular phrase, "chasing" the cure—and even slept outside. (The fashion for screened porches dates to the rise in popularity of altitude therapy.) The mild climates of the southern Southwest were thus especially popular destinations for tuberculars. Dr. Sparks most likely aimed Reverend Cabe and his family towards New Mexico because of the hundreds of tuberculosis sanitoriums that had sprung up in the state and because of glowing recommendations from tuberculosis specialists like Dr. J. F. Danter, a Toronto physician who visited New Mexico territory in 1891. Danter grandly reported that

121

New Mexico was superior "to any other part of the United States or the world in helping to cure the consumptive."

Claims like these propelled hundreds of thousands of "lungers," as tuberculosis sufferers were called, West. The flood of health-seekers began around the 1880s after the railroads made Western travel more comfortable and affordable, and continued until the 1940s, when antibiotics began to be widely distributed. One of every eleven New Mexicans in the early 1900s came to the state seeking a cure for tuberculosis, according to Dr. Ernest Sweet, author of a U.S. Public Health Service study published in 1913 and quoted in *Doctors of Medicine in New Mexico*, by Jake W. Spidle, Jr. (Family members accompanying health-seekers, such as Sarah Della Hope and the couple's seven children, swelled that number considerably.) Like my husband's grandfather, most of the health-seekers were in their twenties or thirties, and most were also men. Dr. Sweet surveyed a thousand health-seekers in El Paso and found 715 men and 285 women. The disease wasn't prejudiced. Women were just as likely to contract tuberculosis as men, but their roles as mothers, wives, and daughters kept them tied down, less able to move West to chase the cure. If Sarah had been the one diagnosed with tuberculosis, would the Cabe family have come West? Most likely not, since that would have meant sacrificing Reverend Cabe's livelihood. But since it was Reverend Cabe who was ill, his income-earning potential was already lost, and so the family might as well chance the move West. They had nothing left to lose.

Tuberculosis was a big business for the desert Southwest, ranking equal in its economic benefits and in the numbers of new residents that it attracted, say historians, to agriculture and mining. Towns competed to attract lungers, advertising their healthful qualities. Hospitals, convalescent homes, and sanitoriums sprang up to serve the flood of lungers. Doctors moved in by the hundreds (incidentally, according to Spidle in *Doctors of Medicine in New Mexico*, greatly improving health care for all New Mexicans). The hotel and boardinghouse trade boomed; rental properties were jammed; lungers even sought sanctuary in auto courts (early motels) and hastily erected "tent cities." According to Sweet's study, anywhere from twenty to eighty percent of the households in New Mexico towns sheltered a tubercular boarder in the early 1900s. Moving and storage companies sprang up to serve the con- *123* sumptive migrants, as did other businesses including, of course, funeral homes. Even colleges jumped on the health bandwagon: Our own New Mexico College of Agriculture and Mechanic Arts, now New Mexico State University, advertised "Health" as one of three reasons to attend the school. In an 1899 advertisement, the school boasted that its site in southern New Mexico was "the healthiest locality in the world," drawing "hundreds of invalids" each year. Indeed, the college's first president, Dr. Hiram Hadley, came to Las Cruces to visit his ailing son and stayed on to lead the fledgling college.

Sadly, the outcome of the Cabe family's journey West was also common. Going West was not an infallible cure-all. Between 1903 and 1912, 1,419 people in Albuquerque died of tuberculosis, according to Spidle, at a rate nearly ten times the national tuberculosis death rate. (Albuquerque's total population at the time numbered just ten thousand people.) Ninety-one percent of those deaths, according to Dr. Sweet, were lungers who had recently emigrated to New Mexico. In other words, for many people like my husband's grandfather, going West was futile. Still, the lungers kept coming. Before antibiotics, no other treatment promised so much hope.

After antibiotics became widely available in the late 1940s, the tuberculosis boom fizzled and was quickly forgotten. Tuberculosis sanitoriums closed their doors or converted to other uses. Doctors specializing in the lunger trade retired or changed their practices. Hospitals converted tuberculosis wings to other purposes. Towns no longer touted themselves as sanctuaries for health-seekers.

One of the first sanitoriums for tuberculosis sufferers in southern New Mexico was established at Dripping Springs, a canyon in the Organ Mountains visible from our house. It is a beautiful site for a health sanctuary. Named for the spring itself, which slides down a smooth channel worn in a rock wall at the canyon's head, Dripping Springs is one of the largest canyons cutting into the Organ Mountains. At its upper end, where the spring is, its bare, red-purple rock walls rise steeply above a narrow valley bottom studded with short, twisted hackberry trees and evergreen oaks. The spring, a gush of water after summer rains or rare winter snows, a clear trickle the rest of the year, is one of only two year-round water sources on the west side of the Organ Mountains. From the cool shade of the valley, some two thousand feet above Las Cruces, the hot desert seems far away.

Dripping Springs has served as a sanctuary of sorts, a refuge from the searing heat of the desert, for millennia. Tools, pottery, and other evidence show that people have sojourned in the Dripping Springs area since at least forty-five hundred years ago, during the time that the pharaohs in Egypt were building the first pyramids, according toMike Mallouf, Bureau of Land Management archeologist. But as far as we know, says Mallouf, there were no permanent settlements in the valley in the 1880s when Colonel Eugene Van Patten, a Las Cruces businessman and community leader, began to build "Mountain Camp," a summer place, just around the corner from where Dripping Springs splashes into the valley bottom.

What Van Patten planned for Mountain Camp is not clear. Starting out as a summer retreat for family and friends, it was later advertised as a tuberculosis sanitorium. But Mountain Camp soon evolved into a different kind of sanctuary, an outpost of elegance and generous hospitality in the harsh expanses of the Chihuahuan Desert. By the early 1900s, Mountain Camp had become a gracious resort, one of *the* places to see and be seen in southern New Mexico, far west Texas, and northern Chihuahua, México. It boasted a lovely stone, two-story hotel and a cluster of more rustic tent cabins, which housed tuberculosis sufferers and their families. The hotel included over twenty guest rooms, a dining room large enough to double as a dance hall, and shady, wrap-around verandas. A contemporary photo of the dining room shows a linen-draped table set with silver, china, and crystal; in the background is an upright piano; above hangs a chandelier. Beautifully landscaped grounds surrounded the hotel and cabins with green lawns, flower beds, an orchard, and even a wrought-iron bandstand. Entertainment included concerts at the bandstand, ballroom dances, and Indian dances by residents of nearby Tortugas Pueblo. The *Rio Grande Republican* carried weekly news about Mountain Camp: details of improvements and additions, reports on weddings and other social functions held at the resort, and names of vacationers and visitors—México's Pancho Villa and Sheriff Pat Garrett of Billy the Kid fame among them.

Franklin Hayner, a Las Cruces lumber magnate who later built his own summer retreat in the lower part of Dripping Springs valley, recalled Sundays at the hotel, when it was fashionable for "belles in flowing skirts and beaus in flowing whiskers" to ride several hours up from town just to take Sunday tea in the dining room with three or four hundred other guests. Van Patten's, Hayner said, was "the showplace of the country side," attracting local and El Paso guests plus "wide-eyed Easterners." Mountain Camp was a favorite destination for students and faculty of the New Mexico College of Agriculture and Mechanic Arts as well. References to "pik-nicking at Van Patten's"—poems, stories, reports of group outings— crop up regularly in the *Collegian*, the college magazine, and the *Swastika*, the yearbook, from the 1890s until the World War I years.

Unfortunately, greed shattered the idyll and, in the end, caused Dripping Springs to be closed to the public for many decades. During the resort's boom years, Dr. Nathan Boyd, a physician and officer of an English company that was organized to build a dam on the Río Grande, summered at Mountain Camp with his wife and family. In 1904, Boyd rented a side canyon from Van Patten to establish his own tuberculosis sanitorium and cash in on the lunger boom. Van Patten built Boyd's sanitorium—perched on stilts because of the steepness of the canyon—a house for his family, and supplied meals from Mountain Camp's kitchen. Then Dr. Boyd discovered that the land description on Van Patten's title erred—it included neither Dripping Springs, Mountain Camp, nor the side canyon containing Boyd's sanitorium. Boyd immediately filed a claim to the whole area. Van Patten refiled. Boyd sued for ownership. The dispute went through the New Mexico courts and all the way up to the United States Land Office and finally the secretary of the interior—twice. Although each jurisdiction reaffirmed Van Patten's ownership of the property, the final time in 1909, Boyd refused to budge or to pay his debts to Van Patten. Finally in 1917, the year before my grandfather-in-law and his family came West, Colonel Van Patten, eighty years old, broke, and worn out, sold out to Dr. Boyd for the sum of one dollar.

Neither elegant resort nor antiseptic sanitorium survived much longer. Boyd, nearly bankrupt from the failure of his dam company, sold Dripping Springs and his sanitorium in 1922. The new owners allowed picnickers for a fee and rented summer cabins, but Mountain Camp never regained its former glamour, the sanitorium closing for good. In 1940, the 242-acre complex went up for sale again. A group of forward-thinking Las Crucens tried to raise the four-thousand-dollar asking price, hoping to open the area as a public playground. Their ambitious plans included restoring the buildings, and constructing picnic units, foot and saddle trails, tennis courts, a swimming pool, and a golf course. They failed to raise the funds. As the tuberculosis boom faded from popular memory, so too did the memory of Mountain Camp and the tuberculosis sanitorium. During World War II, the whole area was leased to the army as part of White Sands Proving Ground, now White Sands Missile Range, and officially closed to the public.

Closed to the public it stayed, until the Nature Conservancy, a nonprofit organization dedicated to preserving plants, animals, and natural communities, bought the whole valley in 1988 and traded it to the federal Bureau of Land Management, which manages the surrounding public land including much of the rest of the Organ Mountains. The Bureau of Land Management had spent the previous decade futilely attempting to find a way to protect the Dripping Springs area—then part of the Cox Ranch, a large family ranch—and re-open it to the public. Finally, with the Nature Conservancy's help, the bureau succeeded. The same qualities that had drawn others to Dripping Springs for millennia also attracted the bureau and the Nature Conservancy: Its rare permanent water source, high elevation, and rocky remoteness make this valley a sanctuary far removed from the harsh desert below and from the metropolitan area creeping near. Not just any sanctuary either, Dripping Springs shelters eight kinds of plants and animals found nowhere else in the world.

The geography of the Organ Mountains is part of what makes Dripping Springs so unusual. Just eighteen miles long by one ridge wide, the Organs are not a big mountain range. Although small in area, they loom large. The Organs are the tallest mountains visible from Las Cruces, rising five thousand feet above the surrounding desert to peaks as high as nine thousand feet above sea level. Their soaring height transforms the Organs into a world far removed from the hot, dry landscape below. Since the average air temperature drops about 4°F with each thousand-foot elevation gain, when the thermometer in our back yard records 106° on a sizzling June afternoon, the mercury is not likely to rise much above 90° in Dripping Springs valley. At the site of Mountain Camp, tucked in the narrow upper canyon around the corner from Dripping Springs itself, the temperatures are moderated further by the shade and thermal mass of the towering rock walls.

Height also equals more moisture. As moisture-laden air rises in order to pass over the range, the air cools and drops some of its water. The Organs thereby snag precipitation that never reaches the lower desert. Las Cruces averages just under nine inches of precipitation per year, while Dripping Springs averages more like fifteen inches. The high ridges above Dripping Springs catch even more, funneling moisture down the chute that feeds the springs. With cooler temperatures and increased moisture, mountain ranges such as the Organs, isolated by the formidable expanses of desert surrounding them, indeed merit the name *sky islands.*

Geology is the other reason for Dripping Spring's uniqueness. Born of a volcanic caldera, the Organs are a bipolar range, split into dramatically different north and south halves. The south part of the range is formed of rock layers spewed forth when the caldera exploded several times some 34 to 33 million years ago. The violent explosions built up layers, two miles thick, of dark, reddish-purple rhyolite and orange-red tuff, which now form the skyline of rounded, hump-backed ridges that characterizes the southern part of the Organs. The north half is as different as can be: a fluted skyline of pale gray rocky pinnacles, the "organ pipes" for which the mountains are named. This half of the Organs is comprised of a nubby kind of granite with large quartz crystals formed when the magma was trapped deep underground and cooled slowly. Its geological split personality gives the Organs a wide variety of soil and landform types in a relatively small area, resulting in lots of different niches for many different kinds of plants and animals.

Some of the species that live on sky islands like the Organs are relics, survivors of more temperate climates during the ice ages several tens of thousands of years ago. As climates warmed and dried, these species survived only in the more clement environments of the mountain slopes and canyons. Over time, some, isolated by the miles of desert between sky islands, evolved into unique species, known only from their own particular island mountain range. Most of these endemic species are plants and small animals. (Large animals and birds are more mobile and therefore less likely to be stranded, more likely to be able to migrate from island to island.) The Organ Mountains, although small in area, are home to an unusually large number of such endemic species: two kinds of land snails, a subspecies of the Colorado chipmunk, a small clump-forming cactus, a nodding cliff daisy, an aster, a figwort, and a spectacular evening primrose.

130

If I were to pick one plant to epitomize the magic that attracts people to Dripping Springs, it would be this last, the Organ Mountain evening primrose. Found nowhere else in the world, these perennial plants epitomize life's astounding ability to adapt to changing conditions. While most desert plants evolved water-saving adaptations as climates dried out, Organ Mountain evening primroses instead staked their survival on growing where the water is. This raises problems. For one—and it is a big one—water is in extremely short supply, even in the Organ Mountains. All of the "streams" draining the Organs, even Dripping Springs downstream from the springs itself, barely deserve that title. They only flow above ground after summer rainstorms or occasional winter snows. But many drainages carry water below ground throughout the growing season. Organ Mountain evening primroses have adapted to take advantage of these underground streams, growing smack in the channels of the half-a-dozen or so larger drainages, between about 5,500 and 7,500 feet elevation. The scarcity of appropriate habitat limits their numbers, the entire population of Organ Mountain evening primroses totals only around two thousand plants.

Not only is water in the Organs, as in all desert mountain ranges, limited, but the supply is erratic, oscillating between long drought and sudden deluge. After months of no rain, intense summer thunderstorms may drop as much as four inches in an hour, transforming the dry stream channels where Organ Mountain evening primroses flourish into roaring flash floods carrying a deadly slurry of rocks, mud, and boulders. Such catastrophic floods alternately scour streambeds to bare rock or bury them under several feet of debris. Most plant life is uprooted or smothered. But Organ Mountain evening primroses survive. Their above ground parts, mounds of numerous flexible stems, may be ripped off, but the perennial part of the plant lives on under the surface of the stream channel, protected from the catastrophic floods. After a flash flood passes and the channel dries out, the roots simply sprout a new crop of above-ground stems.

Their ability to thrive in the catastrophic environment of flash-flood channels is not Organ Mountain evening primroses's only magic. These plants look quite ordinary for most of the year, forming green mounds up to three feet high and twice that across, tinged with rust from a sparse cover of sticky hairs. Then, after the first summer rains, each mound of stems sprouts an abundance of long, pointed flower buds. The buds burst open by the hundreds after dusk on summer nights, revealing huge, lemon-yellow, fragrant flowers. But that is not all. Organ Mountain evening primroses have evolved a food-for-sex partnership with two species of giant night-flying moths.

Plants go to great lengths to avoid inbreeding. Unable to wander around freely and thus to find sexual partners to whom they are not intimately related, plants have evolved a wide variety of tricks to accomplish sex while maximizing the mixing of their gene pool. For instance, evening primrose flowers, including those of the Organ Mountain evening primrose, are designed to prohibit self-pollination. Their stigma, the sticky tip of the female sexual part that collects pollen, protrudes above their stamens, the pollen-carrying organs. The heavy golden pollen grains cannot make the upward leap from stamens to stigma. Organ Mountain evening primroses take the prohibition against self-pollination one step further: They are self-sterile. Fertilization only occurs with pollen from a different Organ Mountain evening primrose plant. Since the blossoms open in the darkness of late evening and each lasts only one night, this makes exchange difficult. Hence, Organ Mountain evening primroses, like many flowering plants, depend on a partner to ensure reproduction.

In order to entice partners, Organ Mountain evening primroses offer food. Like all evening primroses, they have evolved nectar glands, deep inside the flower, that secrete a sweet, honeylike fluid much sought by insects, hummingbirds, and bats. When these nectar-sippers visit the flower to drink, their bodies touch first the protruding stigma, depositing pollen grains collected at other flowers, and then the pollen-laden anthers. As the diners fly from blossom to blossom, they cross-pollinate the flowers.

How do airborne diners find night-opening Organ Mountain evening primrose blossoms? Smell and sight: The flowers broadcast a sweet, come-hither fragrance on the night air. And the blossoms's light color makes them visible in even the faintest moonlight.

Unlike other evening primroses, Organ Mountain evening

primrose nectar is not available to just any nectar-feeder. These unique evening primroses have evolved a pencil-thin, seven-inch-long floral tube, the longest of any evening primrose. A pollinator must possess a very long tongue indeed to reach the sweet food at the base of the tube. Although other nectar-feeders attempt to drink from these primroses, only two kinds of night-flying sphinx moths—big ones—have evolved long enough tongues to sip at the nighttime feast provided by Organ Mountain evening primroses.

When Richard and I learned of the partnership between the rare evening primroses and the giant sphinx moths, we determined to watch this example of evolutionary magic. Thus, one Friday night in early July found us driving out of town and up the creosote-bush-clothed bajada sloping steeply towards the base of the Organ Mountains. Past the gravel quarry and around the north side of Tortugas Mountain, its grassy slopes tinted pale green with new growth, and then onto the washboarded gravel road where the pavement ends, we headed up, up, and up through the desert towards the spare slopes of the Organ Mountains and Dripping Springs. The sun slanted low by the time we reached the preserve gate, which was locked now for the night. The caretakers let us in.

We parked the car in the empty gravel parking lot, unpacked our picnic dinner, walked over to the botanical garden in front of the Visitor Center, and settled ourselves on a low rock wall next to a spring sprouting two huge mounds of Organ Mountain evening primrose. Our perch gave a splendid view westward over the Chihuahuan Desert. Below us, the bajada sloped downhill, stippled with olive-green creosote bush, its even expanse broken only by the rounded, tortoiselike hump of Tortugas Mountain. At the base of the bajada, the Mesilla Valley cut a wide north-south swath through the desert, checkered with farms and orchards. The town of Las Cruces sprawled across the valley, edging towards the glimmering thread of the Río Grande. Past the valley, the desert took over again. Cumulonimbus clouds above West Mesa, across the valley thirty miles away, leaked lavender streamers of rain. A hint of cool breeze trickled down Dripping Springs valley behind us, heralding the beginnings of night.

The two nearby mounds of Organ Mountain evening primrose, each five feet across and three or so feet tall, bore hundreds of thumb-length, slender, sharply pointed flower buds poking up through their leafy canopies. Each bud looked ready to pop. The previous night's flowers were wilted into wads like so many wet tissues.

The air was still warm, the early evening light still bright. Crickets chirped nearby. The humming of honeybees filled the air as they traveled from wildflower to wildflower, their hind legs trailing yellow globs of pollen. Black-chinned sparrow and canyon towhee songs echoed from all around. The sun slipped out from behind the lower edge of the storm clouds to the west, tingeing the slice of sky below the clouds ruddy red.

We watched for the opening of the first blossom, betting on the flower buds closest to the ground, where pools of shade merged. Soon, a lengthwise slit appeared in one bud near the ground. Moments later, the case suddenly split, as if slit by an invisible zipper. One edge of a lemon-yellow petal, freed from its tight spiral in the bud, peeked out like a miniature flag. In a minute or so, the force of the unfurling petals flexed the bud case downward, like a banana peel pushed back. I grabbed Richard's hand and pointed at the bud. He turned to look just as the petals unfurled—the flower was open! Its four lemon-yellow petals slowly unwrinkled and spread into a wide, flat, cross shape. Eight golden stamens with pollen grains hanging off of them stuck up from the center, and a sticky stigma protruded above. Fascinated, we watched for more opening blossoms. Soon, buds were unzipping all over. Within fifteen minutes, we counted seven dozen open blossoms on just one plant!

We were so absorbed by the primroses that we forgot to watch the larger view. Richard looked up just as the sun began to slide below the distant horizon, throwing one last beam of light on the thunderclouds towering over West Mesa. At his exclamation, I looked up just in time to see the sun's orange edge disappear. We turned around as the huge silver disk of the moon rose over the head of the valley. We were silent, awestruck.

135

One by one, the birds quit singing, replaced by hundreds of chirping crickets. Soon a big sphinx moth appeared. I heard it before I saw it. Its two pairs of long, wide wings produced a hum so low it was barely audible as it hovered near my ear. The moth was bigger than I imagined, the size of a small bat. The moonlight picked out the dark, treebarklike marbling on its slowly beating, chocolate and silver-gray wings, and the fur mantling its stout, cigar-shaped body.

The big moth flew slowly over the now-hundreds of open Organ Mountain evening primrose flowers, feeding systematically. It hovered about three or four inches above the center of a flower, its long wings beating to hold it in place in the air while it carefully positioned its wire-thin proboscis, a hollow tongue not much bigger than the diameter of a human hair. The moth aimed the delicate proboscis down the narrow floral tube, then dropped itself down, still hovering, its wings now raised in an acute "V," until part of its weight actually rested on one tissuelike petal. It remained thus, hovering and drinking, for what seemed a long time but was probably actually only ten seconds. Having drunk all it could, the big moth rose ponderously, retracted its foot-long proboscis until only a few inches hung down, and then flew gracefully to the next flower and repeated the whole process. Then on to the next flower and the next and the next. Soon the front of its dark body was dusted with golden pollen. As it hovered and lowered itself over a new flower, its furry body contacted the stigma, delivering its gift of pollen.

136

According to Katie Skaggs, former Dripping Springs naturalist, four species of sphinx moths visit the unique primroses. After many nighttime pollination vigils, Katie concluded that only the two largest species—the rustic sphinx moth and the tomato hornworm moth, both dark-colored sphinx moths with wingspans measuring around five inches—possess proboscises long enough to reach the nectar gland at the base of the Organ Mountain evening primrose's elongated floral tube. Smaller sphinxes try to reach the nectary, but cannot, and so quickly fly on. But the rustic sphinx and tomato hornworm moth can sip the flower's nectar, Katie thinks, and therefore also successfully cross-pollinate the primroses. It is an unlikely partnership.

Indeed, hovering sphinx moths seem improbable. Their wings do not look big enough to lift their stout, furry bodies. Powering their long wings and keeping their heavy body aloft requires an enormous amount of energy, and hence their need for high-sugar food like flower nectar. However, hovering raises an even more difficult problem: heat. Sphinx moths's massive flight muscles cannot operate if they are too cold but, once airborne, the activity of the same muscles generates enough body heat to cook the moth to death. This paradox stumped scientists who once thought—as we all learned in school—that sphinx moths and all other insects are poikilotherms, "cold-blooded" animals that cannot regulate their body temperatures internally, as we mammals do. Scientists speculated that since sphinx moths couldn't warm or cool themselves, perhaps they solved the paradox by flying at dusk or at night when temperatures are warm enough for their wing muscles but cool enough to keep them from stewing. A neat explanation, but it doesn't fit. In summer, late evening air temperatures in the desert are still warm enough that the big moths would quickly overheat when hovering.

Intrigued by the mystery, entomologist Bernd Heinrich attached tiny temperature probes to flying sphinx moths and found that they can indeed regulate their own body temperature. Before taking to the air, sphinx moths shiver by firing the synapses of their flight muscles synchronously so that the wings work against each other, resulting in a great deal of heat but no flight. This warms their flight muscles up to the critical 95°F internal temperature. In flight, when their body temperature quickly rises over 110°, sphinx moths circulate heated blood through their large abdomen, which dissipates heat to the outside air. Heinrich's discoveries forced scientists to re-evaluate their perceptions of insects as "primitive," simple life forms. Life is more sophisticated than we think.

A cool breeze blew downhill past Richard and me in the now-dark garden next to the Dripping Springs visitor center. As the color in the western sky faded to dusky purple, bolts of lightning zig-zagged through a distant thundercloud. Another big moth flew in to hover over the evening primrose plants, stopping at one flower to drink, hovering, and then carefully withdrawing its proboscis and moving on. Coyotes yipped and howled from the ridge behind us. Mosquitoes whined around our ears until a small bat fluttered past in pursuit. Poorwill's low voices called monotonously. A nearby owl hooted softly. A third big moth joined the first two over the blossoms. Darkness claimed the landscape, but still the flowers glowed, lit by the moonlight, and the three big moths flew from flower to flower, continuing the slow dance of life with the Organ Mountain evening primroses.

138

Fortunately for the sphinx moths and for all of us, Organ Mountain evening primroses are protected by Dripping Springs Natural Area. When the Nature Conservancy helped the Bureau of Land Management acquire the unique sanctuary that is Dripping Springs, the two groups agreed to an unusual joint management plan: The Conservancy would provide the biological expertise; the Bureau would be responsible for the day-to-day management. The two organizations, figuring that the best way to protect this one-of-a-kind area was to teach people about it and allow them to enjoy it for themselves, envisioned Dripping Springs as a new kind of sanctuary. A preserve open to the public, it would protect the unique human history and provide a safe haven for the endemic animals and plants.

Much has changed since the heyday of Mountain Camp and the lunger invasion that brought the Cabe family West. The once-elegant hotel is now a roofless ruin; its crumbling rock walls still bear faded wallpaper. The lawns have long since died; the ornate bandstand has disappeared; only a tangle of raspberry canes hangs on as a reminder of the extensive gardens. Boyd's wooden sanitorium building stands empty, its windowpanes broken and its floors rotting, home now to pack rats and the occasional fox. But some things have not changed, for Dripping Springs remains a popular spot. The canyon resounds with the voices of some twenty-four thousand people per year, hikers and birdwatchers and picnickers and strollers, people of all kinds drawn to the verdant sanctuary high above the desert.

One hot spring afternoon, I hiked the preserve with Katie Skaggs, a biologist-turned-educator and the preserve's first naturalist. Katie, a bright, energetic, cheerful woman in her early thirties, had just finished a masters degree in biology education at New Mexico State University when the Nature Conservancy advertised for a naturalist for the brand-new Dripping Springs preserve. Tired of living in town and "teaching biology in a shopping mall," Katie jumped at the prospect. "I'm a field biologist," she said as we walked up the trail to Dripping Springs, a rocky gravel road that once carried stagecoaches and wagon loads of visitors to Mountain Camp and patients to Boyd's sanitorium, "I'm happiest with dirt under my fingernails, working outdoors." So Katie and her family, her husband, Roger, also a biologist, and their two elementary-school-aged sons, moved into the small adobe house next to the visitor center at the lower end of Dripping Springs valley, a dusty half-hour car ride from town. It was the sanctuary they needed. One day a week, the two tow-headed boys would forgo the trip to town for school and help Katie with her work. Sometimes that meant helping to lead nature walks for school classes, sometimes assisting Katie as she studied Organ Mountain evening primrose plants. On her morning run up the valley, Katie said, she usually saw deer; at night, quadrillions of stars spangled a sky undimmed by the glare of streetlights.

For the preserve's first four years, until a school-teaching job lured Katie and her family back to the mountains of southwestern New Mexico, Katie was Dripping Springs's foremost evangelist. She led hundreds of nature walks and gave dozens of talks, and her contagious enthusiasm and love for the place enticed numerous volunteers to help study and protect the unique valley. Katie's vision of the new preserve was never a selfish one. It was not just *her* place. She saw Dripping Springs as a living sanctuary, not just for the Organ Mountain evening primroses, the sphinx moths, or for she and her family, but for everyone. Still, the number and variety of visitors surprised even Katie. At first, she said, the Nature Conservancy and Bureau of Land Management worried about the popularity of the place; they didn't want visitors to love it to death. "After all," said Katie, "it's a preserve, not a city park where you can do just about anything."

It turns out that the Bureau and the Conservancy needn't have worried. Despite its popularity, the preserve has remained pleasantly peaceful. I commented on how little trash I saw, surprising given how many people hike the trail. On weekends it carries everyone from serious hikers to families in their best clothes pushing baby strollers. "That's the magic of this place," said Katie, "people come up here with a good attitude. We rarely pick up litter. We have no paid clean-up crew, and we don't need one." "People," she added, "seem to love this place."

"Something that I have only realized recently," Katie said as we turned back towards the Visitor Center to see if the boys had arrived home from school, "is that people see Dripping

Springs as a 'safe' place. It seems to be just wild enough to offer solace, but not wild enough to be scary. People who might not go to a 'wilderness' feel safe coming here," she continued, "especially women."

We walked quietly for a while. As we crossed the dusty parking lot to the Visitor Center, Katie said, "I think that people really do see Dripping Springs as a sanctuary."

While waiting for Katie, I thought about why we treat Dripping Springs as a sanctuary: Is it the rare occurrence of a permanent spring blessing the parched desert country with its water? Is it the rocky beauty of the place itself? Is it because of the unique species that live here and nowhere else in the world? Just outside the fence that encloses the Dripping Springs Natural Area, the desert grasslands are grazed to bare dirt. Beer cans and plastic bags litter the roadside. Subdivisions are popping up all over. Why don't we treat the rest of the desert as a sacred place also? I looked down the valley. Far below, the Río Grande shimmered in the intense sunlight. The birds were silent in the afternoon heat. The dry breeze ruffling my hair brought no answer.

❧

Richard and Molly and I live in an ordinary sudivision in Las Cruces. Our house faces away from the subdivision's curving streets and the other houses, oriented instead to its large backyard and the view across a nearby field. In the background, dominating the eastern horizon, rise the rocky slopes of the Organs. Almost all of the glass in the house looks over the backyard and the view of the distant mountains.

Unfortunately, when we moved in, all the world passing by had a great view of us too. A cement-block wall surrounded the backyard but was too low to give us any privacy. Past the wall, the dirt road atop the irrigation ditch bank afforded strollers, runners, and bicyclists a panoramic view of our lives as we relaxed on our back patio, ate dinner, worked in the vegetable garden, lounged in the living room, hung out laundry. . . . We felt like an exhibit at the zoo. Beyond the irrigation ditch El Paseo's four lanes carry a constant stream of traffic from roaring semi-trailer trucks to the thumping bass of Friday-night cruisers. (Our subdivision marks one end of the cruising strip.) Even without its noise, the unending stream of vehicles on El Paseo disrupted our peaceful view of the Organs.

Thus, we decided that one of our first remodeling projects would be to raise the backyard wall to gain privacy and quiet. But how high should it go? We didn't want to block the view of the mountains; we did want to remove the traffic in the foreground. After much experimenting with string tied at different levels to mark the top of the new wall, we decided to go up four feet. That would screen foot traffic on the ditch road, and would block out all but the tallest vehicles passing on El Paseo. We hoped that the mass of the cement block wall would also dampen some of the traffic noise.

The project succeeded in ways that we didn't expect. A stream of cars no longer passes in front of our view of the mountains; we see only the very tops of pickups and the occasional big truck. Passers-by on the ditch road can no longer observe the details of our lives. The traffic noise is reduced to a steady background rumble. Best of all, though, is the intangible effect: Our sprawling yard, once a fishbowl open to passers-by, has become an intimate place. The curve of its tall gray walls hugs the enclosed space, inviting us outside to relax, to read, to garden, to entertain, to watch the sunset tint the Organs with a ruddy glow and the stars pierce the dark sky at night. We can hear the world outside, but it no longer intrudes. The quality of this outside space changed once we raised the walls.

Now the yard, intimate and protected, is a part of our house. We landscaped it to emphasize these new qualities. At one end of the backyard, where the curve in the wall is lined with a grove of six gnarled, drooping Mexican elder trees, we killed the bermuda grass lawn, rototilled the area, and scattered desert wildflower and grass seeds. For Molly, we hung a private reading hammock hidden by the drooping branches and the pale-green foliage of the Mexican elders. Now our "wilderness" sprouts wild flowers on its own, surprising us with its color and texture, and is home to an abundance of scurrying lizards, butterflies, and chattering birds. Walking paths will someday wind through the wild area, reaching a small patio enclosed by the grove of Mexican elders. Sitting on a bench there, with the flowering branches of the elders around and the hum of bees on the warm air, the rest of the world seems far away. The wild room is our home refuge.

What makes our yard—or any place, for that matter—a sanctuary is how we treat it. Because we raised the wall, the yard came to seem private, inviting, restful, a place to heal, to retreat from the frustrations and busyness of daily life. Once we saw its sanctuarylike qualities, we began to treat it as one. Soon after the new wall was finished, we held a celebrate-the-yard party, inviting all of our friends to come over for a potluck dinner and hand-cranked ice cream. Along with the crowds of friends and the abundance of food came their goodwill and enjoyment. The happiness of that evening and many subsequent ones continues to bless our yard.

Friends comment about the peace and tranquility of our house and yard. Houseguests end their stays surprised at how restful, how healing, the time has been. We find ourselves spending more time at home. Our house and yard provide a quiet center for our lives, a place of refreshment, solace, with time and space for unhurried reflection, reading, relaxing. The yard, with its mix of wild and cultivated spaces, welcomes wild lives too, from spadefoot toads to roadrunners. What began as an ordinary suburban house and yard is now a refuge, an island sanctuary right in town.

144   In *The Thunder Tree*, Robert Michael Pyle's self-described "love song" to the irrigation ditch nearby where he grew up in suburban Denver, a linear stretch of urban wildness that served as a sanctuary for him and untold numbers of other lives, Pyle writes: "It is through close and intimate contact with a particular patch of ground that we learn to respond to the earth, to see that it really matters. We need to recognize the humble places where this alchemy occurs, and treat them as well as we treat our parks and preserves—or better. . . . Everybody has a ditch, or ought to. For only the ditches—and the fields, the woods, the ravines—can teach us to care enough for all the land."

"There is a balm in Gilead," goes one spiritual, "to make the wounded whole." Gilead has no monopoly on balms. Every place is sacred. The qualities that make a place able to heal us, refresh us, and inspire us are part of every landscape; only our vision fails us. We cannot see the beauty, the sacredness in many landscapes, including this battered Chihuahuan Desert. We treat the Chihuahuan Desert as if it was indeed barren, wild, and worthless. It is easy to see the beauty in a place like Dripping Springs Natural Area, with its thread of water splashing down the dark rocks to green the canyon, its history, and its unique plants and animals. But it is harder to see the magic outside the fence that encloses Dripping Springs. Only if we set ourselves to learning its stories and searching out its beauty—the nighttime opening of *reina-de-la-noche*'s magnificent flowers, the petroglyphs etched on dark rocks, the emergence of thousands of chorusing spadefoot toads— do we come to recognize the Chihuahuan Desert as the sanctuary that it is. Until we do so, we will continue to litter the roadsides and arroyos, to squander the groundwater, to overgraze the once-fertile grasslands, to allow unwise development, to tear down the historical buildings, to ignore the stories and traditions of the viejos who came before us. As long as we treat this desert as a worthless place, its qualities as a sanctuary will elude us. Only when we begin to perceive its sacredness will we find the balm in this Gilead.

❧

On my tour of Dripping Springs, Katie Skaggs led me through the gate at the side of the Visitor Center and along a path to where Dripping Springs's arroyo cuts below the old ranch buildings. She stopped me at the top of a steep flight of steps cut into the arroyo bank. Below us, a lichen-crusted cement dam plugged the arroyo bottom. A rusty galvanized metal swimming pool slide plunged downward in a graceful curve from the side of the arroyo into a stand of cattails. A diving board attached to the top of the dam poised over solid ground. Twisted old hackberry trees shaded new growth of willows, cattails, and other water-loving plants. What had once been a swimming pool ponded behind a dam was now a fledgling marsh, growing in layers of mud, gravel, and sand trapped behind the dam when the arroyo carries loads of rocky debris after summer thunderstorms. A verdant green tangle of vegetation now grew in the old swimming pool.

As Katie talked, I noticed a mounded green plant growing from the solid ground in the shade of the diving board. The plant was about two-and-a-half feet tall with wavy, narrowly oval leaves bearing a characteristic rusty tinge: Organ Mountain evening primrose. The plant was positively bursting with flower buds. I pointed it out to Katie. She nodded her head in recognition and grinned. I grinned back. One of the Organ Mountains's endemic plants was quietly reclaiming its own sanctuary.

Terminus

If there is magic on this planet, it is contained in water.
Loren Eisley, *The Immense Journey*

In the West, water runs uphill towards money.
proverb quoted by Marc Reisner in *Cadillac Desert*

The Río Mimbres, or River of the Willows, in southern New Mexico is an ordinary Chihuahuan Desert river. Its story is that of most rivers in this country: born in the mountains, it dwindles to nothing in the desert.

The Mimbres begins high in the Black Range of the Gila Mountains about sixty miles due north of Deming, New Mexico, fed by scanty winter snows and violent summer thunderstorms. The clear waters of its three forks pour off the high country in arrow-straight canyons, passing through forests of spruce, Douglas fir, and ponderosa pine, and merging in a broad valley. From there, on its way to the desert, the Mimbres runs between dry hillsides sparsely dotted with stunted piñon pines, junipers, and oaks. Along the way, its shallow waters nourish small orchards of apple and pear trees, pastures, gardens, and fields of alfalfa and corn. Scattered wild groves of cottonwoods, ashes, walnuts, and willows shade its wide, cobble-strewn bed. Most of the time, the Mimbres is a small stream, only here in this arid country where a perennial stream of any size is an extravagant occurrence would it merit the label *river*.

Like most Chihuahuan Desert rivers, the Mimbres disappears after it exits the mountains, some twenty miles upstream from Deming. Except in big floods, its scanty flow simply sinks into the desert, vanishing into the thirsty soil of its own channel. Its empty bed, a shallow arroyo marked only by the sparse dotting of small desert willow trees, continues on to Deming and beyond, winding through the desert like a ghost river.

Richard and Molly and I have crossed the Río Mimbres many times on Interstate 10 just east of Deming. The only signs of "river" there are the dusty channels carved in the gray soil of the arroyo—footprints of the long-vanished water— the drooping desert willows growing here and there along the dry watercourse, and the green and white highway signs proclaiming, "Mimbres River." Optimistic highway signs, indeed. The river itself is nowhere to be seen. The tracks of desert critters from lizards to all-terrain vehicles trace its empty bed. Wind-blown, sun-bleached skeletons of tumbleweed pile on the arroyo bottom in ephemeral sculptures. As we speed by with the rest of the traffic on the interstate highway, I am saddened by the dry river bed. Did the river used to run here, bringing life to this part of the ever-parched desert? If so, where has the water gone?

After wading through seemingly endless pages of scientific reports and tracking down historic descriptions of the Mimbres River, I can only partially answer the first question. In the cooler climate of the Pleistocene, the glacial age, ten and more thousand years ago when ice covered much of the landscape farther north, the Río Mimbres did indeed run past what is now Deming, and on south, draining into Laguna Palomas, a shallow lake covering many square miles of what is now a dusty basin in northern Chihuahua, México. But whether the Mimbres has in more recent times regularly wetted the bed of the arroyo now crossed by Interstate 10 is simply not clear. What is clear though, is that, like most desert rivers, the Río Mimbres and its green, fecund ribbon of riverside vegetation have shrunk over the past 150 years, leaving the desert dryer and impoverished. Where has the water gone?

In searching for answers to that last question, I set out to trace what is left of the Río Mimbres, beginning with its end, the place where it dwindles to nothing in the desert somewhere upstream of the bridge over the dry arroyo on Interstate 10. In 1856, Thomas Antisell, surveying a route for the Southern Pacific Railroad through this part of New Mexico, described a junglelike riverbottom woodland at the place where the Mimbres disappears below ground, including "a large collection of fresh standing water in pools or lagoons, surrounded by willow thickets." The description sounds lush and verdant, extravagantly wet, a rarity in this spare desert country. Intrigued, Richard and I took off one sunny February day to see the lagoonlike terminus for ourselves.

Finding it wasn't a simple task. We didn't know exactly where the Mimbres ended. Our topographic maps charted the course of the Mimbres, but the maps didn't make it clear where the solid blue line marking the perennial river changed to the dotted blue line meaning "seasonal flow"—sometimes water. We knew that the end of the river lay upstream of where the two-lane highway running northwest from Deming towards Silver City crossed the still-dry river bed. Our map showed a gravel road running upstream through the desert from there, more or less retracing the river's course after it left the mountains. Thus, on that February day, we turned off the highway onto the dusty gravel road, headed, we hoped, for the end of the Río Mimbres.

At first there was no sign of either river or arroyo in the dry grasslands that we drove through. Then we spotted a shallow valley, sparsely dotted with water-loving trees, creasing the even slope of the grasslands to the north. But still no river.

Past a ranch and the bright green rectangles of its irrigated hayfields, the road abruptly plunged down a small bluff into the valley. An expanse of straw-gold native sacaton grassland, tall as a cornfield in August and much more dense, filled the valley bottom from bluff base to bluff base. Nearby, the gray, bumpy trunks of a cluster of hackberry trees punched through the sacaton, the crooked twigs of their winter-bare canopy still bearing a few clumps of last year's wizened, orange berries. Farther away, a dashed line of willows, walnuts, box elders, ashes, and the occasional cottonwood marked the river channel. Still, we could see no flowing water.

As we drove slowly up the valley, we searched for a way through the truck-high stand of tall grass. After several false starts, we finally found a narrow track that headed for a grove of cottonwoods, the first suggestion of Antisell's lush riverbottom woodland that we'd seen. Down the track into the sacaton, past a small pond surrounded by old willows leaning inward over the water, along a burbling irrigation ditch we headed, sure that we'd found the river at last.

When we emerged from the curtain of sacaton at the edge of the cottonwood grove, we saw that we had indeed found the Río Mimbres—and its end. A raw, recently bulldozed earthen dam several feet high ran right across the river channel, plugging the flow. Below the low dam, the channel was empty, dry. Above the dam, the river pooled, and, siphoned by an open headgate, ran into the irrigation ditch that we'd driven along. The grove of cottonwoods, all old and misshapen, massive trunks slightly askew, circled the pond like sentinels at a gravesite.

Here was the terminus of the Mimbres, but not the junglelike end described by Antisell in 1856. Only the old cottonwoods spoke of abundance. Between their furrowed trunks, where a wild tangle of wolfberry, rose, willow, grasses, and grapevines once grew, the ground was grazed bare. No slender stems of young cottonwoods sprouted to replace their elders. Instead of Antisell's tangle of vegetation, the ground was powdered by countless cow hooves, dotted with Frisbee-sized cowpies.

151

Upstream, the slender ribbon of water meandered down a wide, bare channel, exposed to the glaring sun. Here and there a fat old cottonwood or willow stood alone near the flow, remnants of a once-dense riverbottom forest. Not a sign of life showed in the shallow water except for streamers of brilliant green algae waving gently in the current. Their bright green is deceptive. It signals death—water too warm to sustain insects, amphibians, fish, and the other residents of a healthy river.

We explored a little but soon turned to go, sickened by what we found. The wind blew. A thin haze of cloud had spread across the sky, robbing the sunlight of its warmth. The river burbled down the irrigation ditch. Downstream there was no stream. The dry channel smelled of dead algae.

I stopped on the bare bank at the edge of the pool, stooped down, and picked up two rounded, river-worn cobbles. Their satiny surfaces felt cool, soothing, in my hands. "Let's find a

Río Mimbres rock or two to bring home," I suggested. (I like to collect rocks—nothing fancy, just ordinary rocks—as reminders of special places I've been.)

"A cow chip would be more appropriate," Richard replied bitterly, "since that is where the water goes."

I nodded sadly.

He squatted nearby and ran his hands over the rocks.

We sorted rocks silently, turning their smooth, river-rounded shapes over and over in our hands. We finally picked three, said good bye to the river and its sentinel cottonwoods, and drove away. The small flock of mallards that had flown upstream when we drove in circled and dropped down to land on the pond again.

We had found the end of the Río Mimbres indeed. But not the end we'd imagined.

⌘

When we found the dam and irrigation ditch that nowadays terminate the Río Mimbres, Richard and I found part of the answer to the question of where the river's water goes. But I wanted to know why. For that, I turned to water law. I found a simple but chilling answer.

New Mexico law gives no status to rivers as such. In New Mexico, rivers, streams, and other free-flowing waters have no rights to their own water; as in most arid western states, all flowing waters belong to the state. Water cannot be held as private property, a person can own the legal right to use a certain amount of water but not the water itself. Water rights, however, can be bought and sold like property. In fact, they are not tied to the land.

On what basis does the state grant rights to use this precious resource? "Beneficial use," says the New Mexico

Constitution, "shall be the basis, the measure and the limit of the right to the use of water." Unfortunately, our state constitution's authors neglected to spell out the definition of "beneficial use." Beneficial to who or whom? Beneficial in the short term or the long term? The definitions have been argued ever since. In practice—that is, in court—beneficial use has come to mean essentially any legal use of immediate benefit to humans and involves diverting water from the stream or river.

How much water can be diverted for beneficial use? As much as the river or stream delivers. A publication of the State Engineer Office, which regulates New Mexico's waters, declares "Beneficial use . . . includes all applications of water to a lawful purpose useful to the appropriator and consistent with the general public interest in having water utilized to its maximum." It concludes, "Almost all use of water that benefits the water user is viewed as beneficial." In other words, a stream, spring, or river can be drained dry to fill my taps and flush my toilet, to mine and process minerals, to irrigate crops from alfalfa to chiles, to nurture livestock as diverse as dairy cows and ostriches, and to manufacture anything from computer circuit boards to stonewashed jeans. But letting the water flow down the stream, growing trout and mayflies and turtles and cottonwoods, is not considered a beneficial use.

The dam that now terminates the Mimbres River, shunting the river's entire flow into an irrigation ditch, is thus a legal use of the river's water. It dates to 1883, when that particular claim to the water was first filed. The date a claim to a water right was filed determines the precedence of the current owner when water is in short supply and must be allocated. Under the doctrine of prior appropriation, the guiding principle of

western water law along with beneficial use, the first person
to apply water from a river or stream to beneficial use has a
right to that water with priority over all other uses established
at later dates. First come, first served, then and forever. (Note,
however, that the doctrine of prior appropriation does not
apply to native river users such as fish, river otters, diving
beetles, and willow trees, which were, after all, very much
"first to come.")

When the flow of the Río Mimbres is low, the current
owners of the 1883 water right will get their share of water if
there is enough to satisfy the water rights of those with prior
claims. Later claim holders, called "junior" users in water law
jargon, take their share from whatever water remains after
the "senior" users take their share. Since the flow of water in
desert rivers like the Mimbres naturally fluctuates widely over
the course of the year and from year to year, holding a more
senior water right can make the difference between having
water or not, between growing a crop or not. (The river or
stream, of course, is the most junior user of all, having no
legally recognized right to its own water.) Unfortunately, most
southwestern rivers and streams are overappropriated; that
is, the legally recognized claims add up to more water than
usually flows down the stream or river. In extraordinarily wet
years, all water users get their share. (And there may even be
some left over for the fish and the turtles and the beavers and
the cottonwoods.) But extraordinarily wet years are not the
norm. Hence the dry channel below the dam that now terminates the flow of the Mimbres.

What happens to the water? The story of where the water
of the Mimbres River has gone these past hundred-plus years
is traced in multitudes of worn, legal-sized brown kraft paper

154

portfolios stored in the filing cabinets of the district office of the State Engineer in Deming, New Mexico. The dry legal papers in the files document ownership of the rights to the water of the Río Mimbres, beginning in the late 1800s. The file that details the water right legalizing the earthen dam that today terminates the Mimbres River gives one example of where the water has gone, a story echoed, with individual variations, along each of the Southwest's rivers and streams.

The story in this particular file opens on June 11, 1883, when Israel King began constructing a mile-and-a-half long *acequia* or community irrigation ditch to be supplied by a reservoir (near the current pond) on the Mimbres River. The water for the ditch, according to the records, was diverted from the Mimbres River "and certain springs and cienegas." The files do not detail who bought water from Israel King's ditch, but it seems likely to have been small farmers. At that time, the valley between the Black Range and the Gila Mountains was a breadbasket supplying the mining towns and military forts of the surrounding area with food from fields of grain, corn, vegetables, and fruit orchards. Each field, each orchard, each pasture was watered from the Mimbres River.

Gold fever had hit the area in 1859, when Forty-Niners drifting east from the California gold rush discovered the precious metal at Pinos Altos about thirty miles northwest. The deposits were rich ones, eventually producing ores worth $9.7 million dollars, and spurring a frenzy of prospecting and mining throughout the area. Silver was discovered in the early 1860s at *La Cienega de San Vicente*, soon renamed Silver City, at Georgetown on a tributary of the Río Mimbres in 1866, and just to the south of Israel King's ditch in the Cooke's Peak area in the 1870s. One of the most fabulous silver deposits in the world was discovered across the nearby Black Range in 1879, four years before King commenced digging his acequia. This rich find included the Bridal Chamber, a cavity roughly one hundred feet square, filled with some 2.5 million ounces of "horn silver," ore so pure that the miners simply sawed it into blocks and removed it.

Around the time that Israel King built his acequia, cattle ranching also reached the Mimbres Valley. Huge herds of cattle were driven into southern New Mexico from Texas in the early 1880s. With no fences to restrain them or mark property boundaries, the semiwild herds ranged freely from mountain meadows to desert grasslands. Heaven help the farmer whose fields of beans or melons were in the way! The lush look of the dry grasslands encouraged ranchers to stock wildly optimistic numbers of animals. Within a few years, however, the arid landscape was seriously overgrazed. Cattle prices dropped, and many ranches failed.

Times were hard all around. Between the 1885 and 1905 censuses, the population of the Mimbres Valley plunged as farms failed and farm families moved elsewhere. The price of silver crashed in 1886 and then again in 1891. Mines closed, and only one of the area's military forts remained. The market for Mimbres Valley produce and grain all but disappeared. The tumultuous economic times show in the records of the water right. Sometime during the 1880s—the files do not reveal the exact date—Israel King sold his acequia and water rights to A. B. Spalding, who subsequently sold to the Río Mimbres Irrigation Company, which sold out to G. H. Young, who later sold to the Tigner Ranch. . . .

When the dust settled, a few small farms remained in the Mimbres Valley, but cattle ranching dominated the river and its water for the next six decades (as was true for most of the rural Southwest). The water right that today terminates the Mimbres River stayed in the hands of the Tigner family for several generations, the river's flow going to irrigate hayfields and fill stock tanks. Like many other ranchers in the Southwest, the Tigners built up a substantial spread by acquiring small parcels and water rights along their section of the river. Owning the water gave the Tigner Ranch control over miles and miles of the surrounding waterless public land. In the files documenting the water right is a much-faded map of the Tigner Ranch filed in 1937. It shows a rectangle covering parts of four townships with only a narrow corridor along the Mimbres River marked "deeded land," the acres that the family actually owned. The remainder, hundreds of square miles of desert grasslands, was leased, not owned, public land.

After World War II, things began to change again. The defense industry brought a flood of new residents and jobs to New Mexico, and the hordes of young people who left rural towns, farms, and ranches to help with the war effort didn't necessarily return afterwards. By the 1960 census, New Mexico's population was for the first time more urban than rural. Within a few years of that turning point, another boom hit the Mimbres Valley and the rest of the desert Southwest: a land boom. A southerly flow of retirees eager to leave winter flooded the region. Arid-country land and its scanty water was suddenly valuable for a new crop, subdivisions. Names like "City of the Sun," "Sunshine Estates," and "La Vida del Sol" sprouted on billboards announcing developments in the midst of the sparsely populated desert.

The lure of money to be made in the land boom seems to have cost the Tigner family their ranch. On February 15,

1963, Fletcher C. Tigner filed a "Change of Ownership of Water Right" form affirming that he had transferred his water rights, including the former Israel King irrigation ditch, to the Triple S Land Corporation of nearby Deming. Triple S planned to develop this part of the Tigner Ranch into the "Deming Ranchettes," a subdivision with a recreational lake fed by the Mimbres River. But, like many other developments, Mimbres River Ranchettes went bust. Less than a year after Fletcher Tigner transferred his land and water rights to Triple S, Willie Mae Walsh and the Equitable Life Assurance Society acquired the land and water rights. Instead of filling a "recreational lake," Israel King's water right returned to growing hay and beef.

158

Today, according to the documents in the brown kraft paper files at the district office of the State Engineer in Deming, little has changed. The Mimbres River water flowing down that burbling ditch belongs to Cerro Gordo Ranches, whose owners are listed as Jim Walsh and the Equitable Life Assurance Society. Walsh the younger continues to maintain the dam that terminates the Mimbres River at the century-old grove of cottonwoods. The river continues to flow into the irrigation ditch, watering hayfields and cattle, instead of nurturing fish and filling its own channel. The cottonwoods in the circle around the pond grow fatter and older, closer to death.

Change continues to affect the water of the Río Mimbres, however. More and more users tap the Mimbres's slender flow. The farms and ranches of the Mimbres Valley are being nibbled away by subdivision, split into few-acre parcels for retirement homes, summer homes, and year-round residences. Downstream from the site of Israel King's acequia, a piece of the old Tigner Ranch has metamorphosed into "RV Ranch," a campground and wintering place for snowbirds. Upstream, houses on small "ranchettes" sprout in the hayfields and native sacaton grassland. All claim a share of the slender thread of the Río Mimbres.

What has the last century-plus of draining the river for farming, mining, ranching, and subdivision meant for the Río Mimbres? To answer that question, I dug in the journals of early travelers to the Southwest and discovered the exemplary tale of a small fish.

On October 17, 1846, General Stephen Watts Kearney's Army of the West crossed the Río Mimbres on its way to California, about fifteen miles upstream of the site of the dam that now terminates the surface flow of the Mimbres. First Lieutenant William Helmsly Emory of the U.S. Army Topographical Corps was struck by the lush vegetation. The Mimbres Valley, wrote Emory in his journal, is "truly beautiful, about one mile wide of rich fertile soil, densely covered with cotton-wood, walnut, ash &c [etc.]." The river itself, he described as "a rapid, dashing stream, about fifteen feet wide and three deep . . . filled with trout."

159

Five years later, on April 30, 1851, John Russell Bartlett, chief commissioner to the newly created U.S.–Mexico Boundary Commission, and his survey party approached the Mimbres River from the south. Bartlett's first view of the Río Mimbres so impressed him that he wrote in his journal, "We could discern, far in the distance, a streak of dark green, resembling a huge serpent. Far as the eye could reach, this dark streak wound its way, now expanding into the plain, and again contracting its dimensions among the hills. . . . This was the long-talked-of River Mimbres." Ten miles further along, the party—eight wagons, a number of riding mules, and Bartlett's light traveling carriage—reached the edge of the valley. "The bottom for nearly a mile in width was covered with verdure, such as we had not seen since leaving the rich valleys near Fredericksburg, in [central] Texas," wrote Bartlett.

Bartlett and his party pitched their tents in a cottonwood grove a mile or so upstream from the site of the dam that now terminates the surface flow of the Mimbres. The next day, May 1, Bartlett spent hunting and sketching, first traveling two miles downriver to a thick grove of large cottonwood trees. Here the valley bottom was "thickly wooded and forest-like. Ash and oaks were interspersed among the cotton-woods. Saw many signs of turkeys. . . ." Bartlett noticed "wild roses in great profusion, also wild hops [grapes?], and the Missouri currant." The vegetation was in some places "so closely entangled together that it was impossible for one to work his way through." At the end of that day's entry, Bartlett noted, "A number of fish of the trout species were taken here."

The "trout" collected by Bartlett's expedition and mentioned by Emory were actually Chihuahua chub, a kind of fish unique to the Mimbres River and the once-connected Lago de Guzman basin in northern Mexico. (The Mimbres boasts no native trout species.) The specimens collected from the Mimbres in 1851 by Bartlett's expedition eventually made their way to the Smithsonian Institution in Washington, D.C., and were named by Spencer F. Baird, assistant secretary of the Smithsonian, and his colleague Charles Girard. Because the notes accompanying the fish mistakenly recorded the collection location as "Rio Mimbres, tributary of the Gila,"

Baird and Girard assigned the little fish to the genus *Gila,* commemorating the Gila River. Not only is the Mimbres *not* a tributary of the Gila, Chihuahua chub are not found in the Gila River.

Chihuahua chub are an important clue to what the past century of using the Río Mimbres's water for beneficial use has meant for the river. These small fish—adults grow to around 6 inches long—occupy the niche that trout would occupy in a larger river. Like trout, Chihuahua chub need a river with clear water and with riverside vegetation shading the water and providing habitat for insects and other food. They also require a river bed with deep pools for hunting and sandy stretches for spawning. Chihuahua chub even look like small trout. Their backs and sides are brassy green, their belly is creamy colored, and they blush with orange during spawning season. When Emory mentioned them and Bartlett's expedition collected them, the river must have provided ample habitat as far downstream as the area of the dam that now terminates its flow. The river no longer provides ample habitat. In fact, for much of the year, it barely flows as far as where Bartlett's expedition collected the type specimens of Chihuahua chub.

Beneficial use has been hard on the Río Mimbres and on other southwestern rivers and streams. Exuberant development of the river and the surrounding landscape in the late 1800s drastically changed the river's watershed, river channel, and flow. Mining wastes clogged tributaries, silting spawning beds, and spilled down into the main channel in choking mud and debris flows. (Mine tailings continue to leak toxic pollutants into nearby drainages from some turn-of-the-century mines.) Logging for mine timbers and fuelwood denuded an astounding amount of the watershed. In nearby Arizona, geographers Conrad Bahre and Charles Hutchinson figured that fifty thousand cords of oak, juniper, and mesquite were cut to fuel the stamp mills of Tombstone between 1879 and 1886. Bahre and Hutchinson say that another fifty thousand cords were probably cut to power steam pumps and hoists for the mines, and another thirty thousand cords for domestic uses. The woodcutting during just those seven years, Bahre and Hutchinson figure, denuded woodlands up to twenty-five miles away from Tombstone.

162   Then along came cattle and other domestic livestock. The wild oscillations of the livestock market in the decades around the turn of the century lead to widespread overgrazing. Watersheds already overlogged were grazed bare in places. The steep slopes above the Mimbres eroded quickly. Rains and snowmelt poured off of the watershed, carrying loads of sand, silt, and gravel. River flows fluctuated more and more widely, alternating between flood and drought with less and less "normal" flows in between.

This exuberant development might not have had such disastrous effects on the Río Mimbres if the river system had not already been unbalanced by the effects of a previous boom: beaver trapping. Between 1825 and 1840, trappers like James Ohio Pattie combed the streams and rivers of the Southwest for beaver. In one two-week trapping spree on the nearby San Francisco River, for instance, Pattie claimed that he and his six colleagues trapped an astounding one thousand beaver. So effective were the trappers, say the biologists, that beaver were essentially exterminated in the inland West by 1840. Beaver dams help even out river and stream flows by trapping rain and snowmelt and releasing the water slowly, by keeping water tables high, and by physically stabilizing the soft soils of meadows and riverbanks. Without them, once the watersheds were denuded, all hell broke loose. In 1895, for example, heavy rains poured off of the overgrazed and overlogged hills around Silver City. A twelve-foot-high wall of water tore through town, carving a thirty-five-foot-deep arroyo where Main Street had been. A subsequent flood in 1903 cut the arroyo down to a total of fifty-five feet below the original ground level.

By the 1930s, engineers were using heavy equipment and drastic measures in an attempt to stabilize river systems kicked out of whack by unwise use. On the Río Mimbres, parts of the channel were straightened and levees were built to contain floodwaters. When floods ripped out fords and irrigation ditches, clogged channels with tons of gravel, or cut down below headgates, the channel was bulldozed. For a short period in the 1970s, many old cottonwoods along the river were cut in a misguided effort to increase the flow of water in the now-diminished river. Still, the Mimbres didn't recover.

Today the verdure stretching nearly a mile wide that so delighted both Emory and Bartlett flourishes no more. Groves of cottonwoods survive here and there but they are all old trees, approaching the end of their century-plus lives. In a few decades, these remnant groves too will die and fall. Wild roses, grapevines, and currants no longer tangle in lush profusion in the heavily grazed valley bottom. Even the *mimbres—* willows—for which the river is named no longer line the channel.

The river itself is a ghost of the "lively stream" described by Emory. Its bed is a naked channel in some places a tenth of a mile wide bearing just a slender thread of water a few inches deep. In effect, the Río Mimbres is an aquatic desert. The circle of old cottonwoods around the pond by the dam stands as a poignant reminder of the serpentlike swath of green that greeted Bartlett's party in 1851.

No wonder, then, that by early in the 1900s, Chihuahua chub were no longer found in the Mimbres River. The little fish with the mistaken scientific name seemed to have vanished. But in 1975, Bill Rogers, a high school teacher doing a summer research project, rediscovered Chihuahua chub upstream of the town of Mimbres. Today, a few of the troutlike fish still survive in a three-mile stretch of the Mimbres River, above where the channel and flow have been most changed by beneficial use, and about thirty river miles upstream from where they were originally collected.

Chihuahua chub are important far beyond their size. The little fish are a bellwether species, a miner's canary telling us about the health of the whole Mimbres Valley ecosystem. Even though these fish are uniquely adapted to their desert river, Chihuahua chub cannot survive the devastating floods that scour the deep holes from the river channel and topple the old cottonwoods that line its banks. Nor can the signature fish of the Mimbres survive the bulldozing and channelization of the river bed for flood control and irrigation projects. Nor can Chihuahua chub survive the demise of the tangle of woodland, including the river's namesake *mimbres*, that once kept the water a clement temperature and supplied insect food. And they certainly cannot survive in the dry river bed below where a legal diversion dam sucks away the entire surface flow of the river.

If we lose Chihuahua chub, we will have terminated the Río Mimbres indeed.

❧

The story of the Río Mimbres doesn't end at the dam under the circle of old cottonwoods. The Mimbres is an ordinary Chihuahuan Desert river and, like all desert rivers, it has two lives, one above ground and one below ground. Where does the water go after the Mimbres sinks into the ground, vanishing in the dusty soil of its own shallow arroyo? In searching for answers to that question, I found that the Río Mimbres does indeed reach Deming and still flows as far as México— underground.

Where the Río Mimbres exits the mountains, it enters a basin created when crustal plate crashing around thirty million years ago began to stretch the earth's crust in western North America. The tension caused north-south–trending faults to rip the crust, pushing some sections up and dropping others down. The uptilted blocks form today's small, narrow desert mountain ranges; the downdropped blocks, basins like the Mimbres Basin. Over the millennia since the faults ripped the crust, rivers eroded the upraised mountains, filling the basins with layer upon layer of porous sediments. The result, with the Mimbres Basin and most other southwestern basins, is near-level valleys that resemble the dry beds of giant, shallow lakes and are as porous as sponges. When a river hits the flat surface of a desert basin, except at flood stage when the flow has plenty of momentum, it slows down and sinks into the ground, seemingly vanishing.

Where does the water go? Beneath today's gently southward-tilting basin surface lie two to four thousand feet of sediments from tiny clay particles to boulders. The water from the modern Río Mimbres trickles down into porous layers in the upper several hundred feet of these sediments. Sand and gravel layers carry the underground water while adjacent, comparatively impermeable silt and clay layers confine the water's flow, and act as barriers to its downward or sideways movement. Beneath the desert surface, the Mimbres no longer looks like a river. Instead of running unimpeded in a broad channel, the water trickles along in the minute spaces between the sand and gravel particles, headed inexorably downhill towards México fifty-plus miles south of where the Río Mimbres disappears into its own bed.

Groundwater is hard to picture—we cannot see it. Nor can we measure its volume or flow like that of a stream or a lake. Imagine a gently tilted sandbox with thick layers of plywood pressing on the sand from above and below. Water trickles into the sand from the uphill side, percolates down until it hits the lower plywood layer, spreads out until confined by the sides of the sandbox, and then flows along through the sand just above the plywood bottom layer.

The sands and gravels that carry the water of the Mimbres underground are especially difficult to picture because they are not continuous horizontal layers like those of our sandbox. They are discrete bodies, lens-shaped in cross-section, from five to forty-five feet thick, and longer than they are wide. If you could see through the matrix of silt that buries them, the water-bearing sediments would look very much like schools of giant, lumpy whales swimming southward underground towards México. These odd-shaped sand and gravel deposits are actually ancient, buried river channels deposited by the ancestral Mimbres. During cooler climates of the glacial ages from some 200,000 years ago to as recently as 10,000 years ago, the river carried enough water to flow across the desert above ground and to drain into Laguna Palomas, an extensive shallow lake in northern México. In those wetter millennia, the Mimbres moved its channel here and there across the desert floor, leaving behind the sand and gravel deposits, today buried, that carry the river's underground flow.

Whether the Río Mimbres has, in more recent times than the distant Pleistocene, ever regularly flowed on the surface as far as Deming is unclear. But, according to historical accounts, the underground flow once was close enough to the surface to nurture wet spots in the overwhelmingly dry expanses of the Mimbres Basin. In mid-April 1852, Dr. Edgar A. Mearns, a surgeon-naturalist who worked for the U. S. Boundary Survey, collected water birds at one of these oases, Lake Palomas, a shallow lake and cienega, marshy area, just south of Columbus at the south end of the Mimbres Basin. In 1914, U.S. government geologist N. H. Darton described areas in the lower parts of the basin where "thick deposits of relatively impervious clay" held rainwater at the surface in seasonal ponds. Darton noted that the groundwater came very close to the basin surface in places, creating cienegas. A map in his report shows one such area, labeled "Florida Lake," where the now-dry channel of the Río Mimbres passes around the north end of the Florida Mountains. Today the cienegas and seasonal wet areas noted by Mearns and Darton are gone. Florida Lake has disappeared. Lake Palomas is usually dry; its bed takes to the air in stinging dust clouds when the wind blows.

Where has the water gone?

Uphill towards money. The discovery in the late 1800s that water trickled just under the surface of the bleak desert brought the Southern Pacific Railroad and a flood of settlers to the Mimbres Basin to tap the groundwater.

Deming, the largest town in the lower Mimbres Basin and the county seat, was founded by the railroad in 1881 at a place where the now-dry arroyo of the Río Mimbres curves around the northern end of the Florida Mountains. Shallow wells drilled by the railroad there yielded abundant fresh water, and the word spread quickly: There was water under the desert, water enough to make the desert green. Deming quickly grew from a tent camp for railroad workers to a real town with streets, sidewalks, and adobe, frame, and brick buildings. By 1902, the town and its "forest of windmills" had grown substantial enough to impress Monsignor Henry Granjon, the Catholic bishop of Tucson, who traveled through on a pastoral visit. (Back then, each home or business erected its own windmill to tap the groundwater.)

The seemingly endless supply of underground water in the lower Mimbres Basin attracted merchants, land speculators, well drillers, and, of course, farmers. Deming's boosters trumpeted the virtues of the area—year-round sunshine, few insect pests, and, most important, abundant, pure water. A promotional postcard from 1915 shows a well pouring a torrent of clear water into an irrigation ditch and boasts, "Population 10,000. Watch us grow!" Irrigated agriculture boomed. Geologist Darton reported in 1914 that nearly two hundred wells tapped the underground flow, nourishing some twenty-thousand acres of beans, vegetables, melons, grains, and hay in the desert around Deming.

The agricultural boom went bust during World War I. But the dream of water with which to green the desert didn't die. After World War II, a combination of the prosperous post-war economy and improved pumping and drilling technology revived the boom. By 1969, sixty-two thousand acres of the Chihuahuan Desert around Deming and south were plowed for crops like cotton, wheat, and sorghum, all dependent on Mimbres Basin groundwater.

While the acreages of farms watered by groundwater increased, the supply of water did not. Beginning in 1910 to 1920, the first decade that well levels were monitored, groundwater levels began dropping. (The well level is the height that water rises in the well pipe, pushed upwards by the pressure of groundwater flow. Well levels normally plummet in spring and summer when pumping is greatest, and recover when pumping slacks off in winter.) Well levels in the lower Mimbres Basin have dropped an average of one-and-a-half feet each year since 1910. In the areas of heaviest irrigation, well levels have fallen more than one hundred feet since pumping began.

We don't know exactly how much water there is in the aquifers supplied by the Río Mimbres and the arroyos that empty into the basin. Measuring the amount of water held in discontinuous, buried layers of sand and gravel is not as simple as measuring the volume of a lake or the flow of a river. (Imagine trying to measure the amount of water in numerous odd-shaped sponges buried underground.) In 1917, geologist Darton estimated the amount of groundwater in the Mimbres Basin at 2.5 million acre-feet. (An acre-foot is the amount of water necessary to cover an acre of land one foot deep.) He figured that the aquifer was being recharged at an infinitesimally slow rate: less than half an inch per year. Computer modeling promises someday to yield a more precise understanding of how much water lies under the Mimbres Basin, but Darton's rough estimate still remains a good guess.

If groundwater supplies are being recharged at an average rate of just half an *inch* each year and well levels are dropping by an average of one-and-a-half *feet* in the same time period, the result is a considerable yearly deficit. It looks like we are managing the groundwater of the Mimbres Basin about as well as we are managing the federal budget. Not surprisingly, the State Engineer Office, responsible for managing the groundwater of the Mimbres Basin since 1931, closed the lower Mimbres Basin to applications for new groundwater rights in the early 1940s. Still, well levels continue to drop.

170   Why? The water under the desert of the Mimbres Basin has been managed as a finite resource on the assumption that it will be used up someday. Further, the State Engineer Office has no way of tracking how much water is actually pumped since groundwater wells are not metered. Permits for agricultural wells, for example, simply specify the amount of acres that can be irrigated, assuming a set rate of three acre-feet per acre per year. In other words, even if we knew how much water lies beneath the surface of the lower Mimbres Basin (we don't) and even if we knew how much was added to that supply each year by the slender flow of the Río Mimbres and the seasonal arroyos that empty into the basin (we don't), we still don't know how much of that water we use each year.

Who uses the underground flow of the Río Mimbres today? Farms. Of 926 permitted wells in the lower Mimbres Basin from north of Deming to around Columbus on the international border, nine hundred irrigate crops. (This number does not include wells supplying individual houses and stock tanks, which are deemed too small to require a permit.) The remaining twenty-six wells supply the town of Deming, the village of Columbus, and local industry, including the

Deming bottled water company. In 1990, the latest year for which figures are available, the area used a total of 108,796 acre-feet of water, enough to flood 170 square miles of land—more than half of the area of New York City—one foot deep. Over ninety-five percent of that watered farm crops. (Agriculture is the biggest water user in New Mexico. In 1990, farms and ranches accounted for seventy-nine percent of the water used, in contrast to domestic supplies for the state's 1.5 million people, which accounted for just eight percent.)

Food production is important—we all eat. But it can't come at the cost of using up our scarce water. Most fields in the lower Mimbres Basin are watered by flood irrigation, where the water is poured onto the fields and stands until it soaks in, or evaporates. Here in the Chihuahuan Desert, experts say that half or more of flood irrigation water may evaporate, depending on the weather conditions. In a recent report, engineer Brian C. Wilson estimated that nearly two-thirds of the groundwater pumped from the lower Mimbres Basin in 1990 evaporated or was otherwise not returned to the aquifer. Agricultural uses accounted for ninety-six percent of that depletion.

The neighborhood where Richard, Molly, and I live boasts emerald green lawns and leafy shade trees. This artificial oasis is maintained only by regular watering. After we bought our house, we replaced two-thirds of our water-hungry lawn with desert vegetation supplemented in places by drip irrigation. Water conservation is not yet a concern for most of our neighbors or the city of Las Cruces. Why should we care? In 1990, according to Wilson's report, ninety-two percent of the water used in Doña Ana County was used by agriculture. The county's 120,000 residents used just five percent of the total.

The effects of dewatering the aquifers, of using up groundwater, are more subtle than the effects of drying up surface rivers and streams but no less profound. Aerial photographs of the lower Mimbres Basin are marked by dozens of cracks splitting the level surface of the basin. Each surface fissure is hundreds to thousands of feet long. Some look like jagged lightning bolts, others branch like cottonwood trees. Up to ten feet deep and thirty feet wide, these arroyos in the making are new—they began appearing in the mid-1950s—and, say the geologists who study them, a result of intensive groundwater pumping. The oldest fissures occur near the center of the 350-square-mile area where well levels have dropped the most; new fissures continue to appear towards the edges. Although they resemble arroyos eroded by gully-washing rainstorms, these gullies are created by too little water, not too much. They are subsidence cracks, fractures in the flat basin surface that occur when sediments beneath settle.

As water is pumped out of the loosely packed sand and gravel layers, they compress, sagging downward. Measurements of survey benchmarks and irrigation well platforms show that the surface of the basin has sunk perceptibly, especially since groundwater pumping accelerated after 1950. At one benchmark, the ground subsided eleven inches between 1953 and 1980. Irrigation wells drilled in the 1950s sit on cement slabs originally flush with the ground. The slabs now protrude twelve to fifteen inches above the surface! Parts of the lower Mimbres Basin have sunk over a foot and a half in the past forty years. As the surface sinks, it tears, forming the fissures. The deep earth cracks have already ripped through roads and irrigation canals, caused the abandonment of a home where an active fissure runs to within two feet of its foundation, and could break gas and water lines.

Groundwater pumping is also "desertifying" the lower Mimbres Basin, making the desert dryer. Deserts come in varying shades of dry, from Saharalike sand dunes to near-tropical cactus "forests." As the groundwater has dropped deeper and deeper below the surface, the seasonal wet areas noted by Mearns and Darton have dried up. Even the sparse shrub cover may be a symptom of a desert growing dryer, changing gradually from an arid grassland to a less-verdant shrubland.

Another, more subtle form of desertification may also result from farming based on groundwater pumping. In the lower Mimbres Basin, up to a third of the plowed fields sit unwatered and bare in any given growing season, their three-acre-foot-per-acre-per-year allotment of groundwater "borrowed" to water crops in other fields that need additional water. Although boosters of agriculture once proclaimed optimistically that "rain follows the plow," it turns out that in arid climates like the Chihuahuan Desert, drought is more likely to follow the plow than rain. Research by Kenneth Kunkel, a climatologist who studied Midwest farmlands during the devastating 1988 drought, shows that plowed, bare fields can actually intensify regional drought conditions. Local rainfall is dependent in part on local soil moisture. Bare fields store more heat than unplowed, vegetated fields and dry out more quickly, thus returning essentially no moisture to the local air and making rain less likely in dry conditions. The balance between a habitable desert and an uninhabitable one is delicate, resting on very small amounts of water.

❧

The Río Mimbres reaches its final end in the scrub desert near Columbus, a village of some seven hundred residents on the international border, forty-five air miles south of where the dam ends the river's surface flow. On a farm near Columbus, pumps suck the underground water supplied by the Río Mimbres up from deep beneath the desert and pour it out onto fields. In a terrible irony that exemplifies all of the contradictions of water use in arid country, excess irrigation water runs off the fields into the desert, creating ponds and marshy areas that attract wildlife like the natural wetlands once did. This is a crazy world indeed: we dry out the desert's cienegas by mining the groundwater; then we pour that precious water out on the desert, creating artificial wet areas that will last only as long as the finite supply of groundwater.

Richard and I set out for Columbus one winter weekend to investigate a report that a flock of several thousand sandhill cranes and at least as many snow geese wintered there. Sandhill cranes once wintered all up and down the Río Grande Valley in New Mexico, but are now as uncommon in southern New Mexico as marshes are. As we drove through the desert east of Columbus, we spotted great swirls of birds rising in the air over distant farm fields. Driving closer, the tiny black dots in the sky resolved themselves into the wide-winged, long-necked and long-legged forms of sandhill cranes. When we reached the first field, we stopped the car by the side of the road, astonished by the sight of hundreds of sandhill cranes. We rolled down the car windows for a better look. The chill wind blowing in brought us the purring, throaty murmur of a multitude of sandhill voices. Cranes picked their way delicately between the rows of straw-colored milo stubble; cranes probed the soil with spearlike beaks, searching for insects and seeds; cranes jumped and bowed on long, graceful legs; cranes bent their long necks to preen iron-gray feathers; cranes took to the air on wide wings. . . .

Our informant directed us down a farm road across the fields towards what looked like a cienega. Where, we wondered, was the water coming from to maintain crane wintering habitat in this dry-as-dust desert? No perennial springs or streams grace the desert for miles around. Past two fields, we bumped up onto a low dike. Beyond it was a small floodwater pond. Past the pond, a track headed along the next field towards the startling green of a large marshy area about a mile north. More cranes and geese circled high in the air above it. In front of us a raft of a dozen or two cinnamon and green-winged teal, small "dabbling" ducks, floated the wind-ruffled water. Here and there between fields stood the rusty metal bodies of gasoline-powered water pumps. This unlikely oasis in the Chihuahuan Desert is created by water pumped out of the aquifer supplied by the Río Mimbres—water from wells whose levels have dropped as much as eighty feet in the past forty years.

The practice of allowing tailwater, excess irrigation water, to flow off fields onto the desert is considered a "waste" of water. It is illegal under New Mexico law. Efficient irrigation requires that tailwater be recaptured and pumped back onto the fields. The thick file on this particular set of wells in the district office of the State Engineer in Deming is jammed with memos, field notes, and photographs documenting what appears to be years, perhaps decades, of tailwater overflow. The well water has certainly been flowing onto the desert for enough seasons to grow marsh-loving plants, for enough years to attract wintering flocks of cranes and geese. The State Engineer Office wants the water overflow stopped.

"Waste" and "efficiency" are trickster words, each laden with an implied value judgment. We say that it is a "waste" of water to let it run off of the fields and pond on the desert where it creates marshy areas, because we mean to say that we value the crops produced with the water more than the wildlife it would otherwise nurture. Yet we don't consider flood irrigation itself a "waste" of water although, in the desert, flood irrigation wastes enormous amounts of water to evaporation.

We say that "efficient" farming means recovering the tailwater and pumping it back on the fields because we mean to say that our vision of farming values maximum crop production, not growing crops in a way that harmonizes with or even enhances the landscape, the community of wild lives to which we belong. Pueblo Indian farmers once welcomed the cranes to their fields, believing that the birds brought good luck. Indeed, probing the soil with their long bills to snatch up insect larvae, sandhill cranes act as natural pest controls, eating insects that may harm next year's crops and enriching the soil with their droppings. "Efficient" farming, on the other hand, teaches us to see the cranes and the other wildlife as "weeds," as competitors, not partners.

Curious about the marshlike areas and the wintering cranes, I called Lauro Guaderrama, the owner of the farm near Columbus, to ask if I could talk to him.

On a spring morning that was already hot at nine o'clock, Lauro, a tall, slender man with receding silver hair and a courtly manner, welcomed me into his house. After we settled into the cool shade of his enclosed back veranda, I told him about my delight at discovering the sandhill cranes on his farm the previous winter.

Lauro nodded and said pleasantly, "I hate the cranes. They eat my wheat—I lost about 50 acres of winter wheat to them last winter."

Startled, I asked him what he planned to do about the cranes.

"Nothing," he said. "I always plant extra acres for them."

What about the water that we saw ponded on the desert outside the fields, I asked, creating the marshy areas? It is, Lauro said, "stored" water that he uses to irrigate his onion fields in the winter. He has, he said, been storing irrigation water that way for twenty years.

"If you hate the cranes," I asked, "why store water that way? You know that the marshy areas that you create attract the cranes and other wildlife. Wet areas are rare in the desert these days."

Lauro nodded. He was silent for a moment. When he spoke, his words were soft, as if he spoke to himself. "It is like a sanctuary for wildlife, isn't it?" he murmured, and smiled.

"Is that what you intend?" I asked.

"The farm is for sale," he said. "I don't make the decisions anymore. I've got it leased to a vegetable and fruit broker. We grow whatever is good for the market."

I asked what he grew. Lauro walked over to a nearby desk, found a computer-printed spreadsheet, put on his reading glasses, and read off the names of about two dozen crops from onions and melons to rapini, a mustard relative used for a salad green. He went on to tell me about growing up in a farm family down the Mesilla Valley near La Union, and talked about how he had built up his three-thousand-acre farm slowly since he bought the original acres in 1953. He was clearly proud of his farm.

Whether or not Lauro Guaderrama is intentionally creating marshes in the desert, he is no more a hero than Delbert Utz, the supervisor of the basin for the State Engineer Office and the one charged with stopping the waste of water, is a villain. It is not that simple. Lauro may dump his tailwater on the desert in a way that attracts cranes and other wildlife, but the water with which he greens this oasis in the desert comes from a declining aquifer. Someday it will be gone and the artificial cienegas will dry up. Delbert, charged with enforcing the water-use laws, is aware of the terrible irony: Whether or not he is successful in preventing Lauro from wasting scarce groundwater, the wet areas and their cranes will eventually vanish, leaving the desert diminished.

Where should the water of the Río Mimbres go? What is "beneficial" use? Growing crops like Lauro's milo, onions, winter wheat, corn, carrots, watermelons, chiles, and cabbages? Or nurturing cranes, geese, ducks, toads, dragonflies, bats, and mosquitoes? Who has the "prior appropriation" in this case? The desert's wild critters, who were here first, or we late-coming humans?

One hot summer night recently, Richard and I had settled into bed when a disturbing noise sounded outside the sliding glass door that opens onto our courtyard. "Thud-skritch," then a pause, "thud-skritch," then a pause, "thud-skritch" . . . We pulled up the shade and shined a flashlight through the glass. There, caught by the light, was a small spadefoot toad, a sapito, its big eyes bulging, pressed right up against the door. He—his jewel-bright colors gave away his gender— was lovely, his glossy black back marbled with glittering dribbles of gold, his eyes yellow with vertical, catlike pupils.

The toad must have dug out in response to the thunder that afternoon, expecting water. But the thunder hadn't been accompanied by rain and, indeed, we hadn't had rain in months. Perhaps the glass of the sliding door, reflecting the bright moonlight, lured him over to try to hop into its "pond." We knew that he would dehydrate quickly if he didn't find a puddle, and after weeks of record-breaking heat and no rain, there were no puddles. We would have to make one. I went to the kitchen and got a glass of water while Richard caught the spadefoot. I poured the water in a depression at the base of a wisteria vine in the courtyard. Richard gently placed the little toad in the temporary puddle. The spadefoot hunkered down immediately, his bug eyes watching us. I went inside and got another glass of water and poured it over the toad. He sat motionless, soaking up water. We watched him for a few minutes. He didn't even blink.

179

"We've done what we can for you, buddy," I said at last. We went inside and back to bed. The next morning, both toad and water were gone, leaving no trace.

We use water carefully in our household, mindful that what we consume isn't available for somebody else—animal, plant, or whomever. But in the case of this spadefoot toad, there was no question in our minds about the correct thing to do: share our water. After all, our water belongs to the toad too. We are neighbors.

Where should the water of the Río Mimbres—and all of the desert's other slender, life-giving streams and rivers—go?

Water use in the desert doesn't have to be a question of either me or you, either cranes or farms, of who can outcompete whom. "Survival of the fittest through competition to the death" turns out to be a poor motto for life, a wrong-headed interpretation of Darwin's theories of evolution. We are now learning that cooperation in nature is just as much the rule as competition. Harris' hawks cooperate to hunt jackrabbits, chasing one rabbit in relays, thereby increasing their hunting success. Honeybees cooperate to find flower nectar and make food for their colony. Whales cooperate to raise their young. Cooperation instead of competition could give us farms that use water wisely *and* water-dependent wildlife. It could give us rivers—with Chihuahua chub—*and* ranchers, miners, small farmers, and other water users.

That is my hope as I think of the Río Mimbres, an ordinary Chihuahuan Desert river flowing quietly from mountains to desert and then underground: that we all learn to cooperate, to live as neighbors. As we find ways to live within the desert's slender provenance, as we learn to act as if we are truly a community, sharing the desert equally with all of our neighbors, plant and animal, human and not, I imagine that the desert will begin to bloom again. It will slowly recover its capacity for beauty and magic. In my vision of the future, the grasses gradually reclaim the bare soil; the marshes return to sparkle in the hot sun; the beavers recolonize the rivers and streams, restoring wetlands behind their elegantly engineered dams; the grizzlies again venture out of the mountains to dig for bulbs in spring; the green serpent of forest lining the Río Mimbres again winds across the desert, home equally to Chihuahua chub and humans. We will all be enriched.

I look forward to that time.

Going South

I have been a stranger in a strange land.
Exodus 2: 22

By the rivers of Babylon,
Where we sat down,
And there we wept,
When we remembered Zion.
How can we sing the Lord's song
In a strange land?
Psalm 137

It is a cold Sunday morning in December, just before dawn, and my friend Denise and I are headed for the village of Tortugas to join the annual pilgrimage for the Fiesta of *Nuestra Señora de Guadalupe*, the Virgin of Guadalupe. Every year, the people of the village, plus outsiders who wish to join them, trek three miles from their church to the summit of Tortugas Mountain. The day atop the mountain is a mix of social and sacred activities. Whole families, from tiny babies to wizened *viejitas,* make the climb, bearing images of the Virgin as well as picnic coolers and lawn chairs. People attend an open-air mass, share food in circles around small cook fires, socialize, and make *quiotes,* carefully decorated walking staffs carved from dried sotol flower stalks gathered from the desert nearby. A smudge fire of green creosote bush branches bathes the mountaintop and the crowd of people in purifying smoke.

When the last pilgrims descend the mountain at dark to return to the village, *luminarias*, bonfires, are lit along the trails leading down the mountain. First a large pile of old tires is lit atop the mountain, and then one by one, beginning at the top, glowing points of orange flame appear along the trails, outlining the small mountain with their light. The whole ceremony is a beautiful connection between faith and landscape. Denise, from a Mejicano family that has lived in the Mesilla Valley for four generations, makes the pilgrimage every year. When she invited me to join her, I was excited and moved.

The sky is light by the time we drive into the narrow lanes of the village that Sunday morning. The white-plastered tower of the church is lit by strings of lights. A large five-pointed star, outlined in blue light bulbs, soars from the roof. I park across the street from the church, and we climb out of the truck sleepily, quickly putting on more layers of clothing as the cold predawn breeze hits us. I strap on a waist pack filled with snacks, water, and sunscreen. Denise pulls on her similarly loaded knapsack.

"Let's go over to the church first," says Denise.

We walk across the neatly raked dirt churchyard and step through the open doors. Inside, the church is brightly lit and warm. Denise stops just within the door to the sanctuary, touches the sponge in the holy water receptacle with her fingers, and crosses herself. I touch the sponge, too, and respectfully imitate her movements. The small church is plain, with white-washed walls and simple stained-glass windows. Up at the front, to the right of the altar, the statue of the Virgin, *Nuestra Señora de Guadalupe*, sits on a platform decorated with intricate rows of lace and ribbons. Several people kneel nearby in prayer.

Denise is restless. "Let's go up to the Casa del Pueblo," she whispers. "We don't want to miss the beginning of the pilgrimage."

We walk back out into the cold and up the quiet street to the Casa del Pueblo, the small adobe community hall. People are gathering there already. Small groups of people walk down the still-dark streets towards the hall; arriving cars disgorge yet more people. All are bundled up warmly against the cold. A few wear Mexican-Indian–style wool ponchos, and some are dressed in fancy ski jackets, some sport black football jackets and baggy pants. Many carry images of the *Virgen*—carved and painted retablos, framed pictures, or scarves printed with her likeness. Everybody seems to know everybody, greeting one another enthusiastically despite the early hour, hugging and shaking hands, and talking and laughing as they load small coolers or knapsacks with food and water. As we thread through the crowd, people here and there reach out to greet Denise, a native and now a successful performance artist, playwright, teacher, and novelist.

We slip inside the crowded community hall, register for the pilgrimage, and buy *veladoras*, tall votive candles in glass jars, to carry up the mountain and place on the altar at the top.

Outside, the sky is light and a crowd of several hundred people has formed in front of the small Casa del Pueblo. Several older men, carrying willow staffs trimmed bare but for a feathery tuft of twigs and leaves atop each staff, begin forming the crowd into two lines. These men are *capitanes de la guerra*, or war captains, the ceremonial leaders of the fiesta. Women line up on the left, men on the right. Denise, Dierdre, a friend of Denise's who has joined us, and I fall into the lefthand line. As soon as the twin lines are formed, the capitanes lead us, walking slowly, two-by-two in each line, back down to the church. We chat quietly as we walk. Late-comers join the lines, swelling the pilgrimage. We file into the warm church, crowding together to fit into the aisle, and the talking stops. Hand after hand touches the holy water sponges and makes the sign of the cross as we shuffle forward towards the statue of the *Virgen de Guadalupe*. Each person stops in front of the Virgin. Some kneel; some bow; all cross themselves and salute Our Lady, perhaps saying a private prayer. We shuffle forward, Denise and Dierdre ahead of me, until it is my turn. Unsure of what to do but wanting to show my respect, I cross myself and bow my head, then move on, pushed by the crowd, until I am expelled again into the cold dawn air.

184

We walk slowly in our orderly lines back to the Casa del Pueblo. Although cold, I am too caught up in the ceremony to mind. In the vacant lot across the street from the small adobe building, the leaders direct us to form a huge circle. The four war captains, only their leafy willow staffs distinguishing them from the rest of the crowd, enter the circle. One carries a beautiful glazed clay pot. A fifth man, the head war captain, walks into the center of the circle and greets us, speaking first in Spanish and then in English.

He thanks us for joining the pilgrimage and reminds us that the people of Tortugas have been trekking to Tortugas Mountain like this "for centuries." The mountain, he says, is sacred to the village and they hope to keep it that way. "Please pick up any trash that you see," he continues. "We don't want our mountain littered with trash." After a few more words about the pilgrimage, the head captain signals to the man carrying the clay pot, and he steps forward. Using an ordinary stainless steel slotted spoon, this second man lifts a few glowing coals out of the pot and offers them to the head captain, who touches a short, fat hand-rolled ceremonial cigarette to the coals, puffs for a moment, and then says, "We will now bless the four directions." He asks us first to turn to the North. We do, and he blows smoke to the north, saying "To the North, for the Father, the Son, and the Holy Ghost." Then he asks us to turn to the West. He blows smoke in that direction and repeats the blessing. Then to the South and, finally, to the East. Afterwards, he blesses our journey. Then the other war captains, carrying their willow staffs, form us into two lines again, and off we walk, headed for Tortugas Mountain.

185

The twin lines of marchers wind slowly across the vacant lot. When we reach the frontage road that runs along Interstate 10, we turn right. A county sheriff's car, its lights flashing, creeps along in front of the mass of people; another blocks the road where the walkers turn onto the pavement. The pilgrims string out along the frontage road like two black ribbons. As we walk, I wonder what the people in the stream of trucks and cars rushing by on Interstate 10 think of the sight of the walkers, some bearing tall yucca staffs, some carrying pictures of the Virgen de Guadalupe. Our slow pilgrimage does not belong to their hurried world. We must present quite an odd picture indeed on this cold Sunday morning as dawn breaks.

People chat and laugh as we walk down the road. The sun rises and disappears behind a layer of high clouds in the southeastern part of the sky. I remember that I am wearing the beautiful Virgin of Guadalupe pin that Denise gave me, and I turn to show it to her and Dierdre. As they admire it, one of the women behind us catches sight of the striking pin. She exclaims, and I turn around while walking to show it to her. A small knot of women gathers around, without breaking the pace, to admire the pin. "Where did you get it?" asks one woman. I say proudly that Denise gave it to me and that her cousin made it. We laugh and talk with the group of women for a few more minutes, then re-form our two-by-two line. As we walk on, I feel less a stranger and more at home.

Soon we turn off of the highway frontage road and scramble down a steep bank into Tortugas Arroyo, the dry streambed that we will follow part way to the base of the mountain. We

pass under the noisy bridge that carries Interstate 10, and we are back in the desert. A drooping desert willow tree hangs over the arroyo bed, its long weathered pods still shedding seeds with their feathery, silken parasols. The sand in the arroyo bottom is soft and the air is beginning to warm up. I unzip my jacket. Dierdre takes off her sweater and stuffs it into her waist pack. Denise takes off her hat. We walk and talk, keeping to our place in the long lines of marchers. We barely notice the university buildings as we pass them. We are in our own world, part of a ceremony older than they are.

Ahead of us are two dark lines of people with one war captain walking solemnly at the front of each. Behind us, the lines stretch for perhaps a half mile down the arroyo like two dark serpents inching slowly uphill through the desert. Groups of pilgrims pass us, carrying coolers and water bottles and yucca staffs, the kids laughing and chasing one another. We are all bound for the same place, the small humpbacked mountain that rises smack in our path, marked with the bold white "A." The sun comes out like a benediction. I feel a surge of joy and pride at taking part in this ceremony. It is a demonstration of faith that seems to me rare and altogether precious.

My mind wanders as we walk. I listen to the soft murmur of voices around me and hear more Spanish than English. In a sea of warm olive, café-con-leche, and mahogany faces, I see only two or three Anglos like me. But despite my obvious foreignness, I feel embraced by this community of faith. As we all walk slowly towards Tortugas Mountain, I realize that participating in this pilgrimage is bringing me closer to this difficult Chihuahuan Desert country. My roots are growing in this dry, gritty soil. It feels good.

When Richard, Molly, and I moved to Las Cruces, I was tired of moving, of the rootlessness that comes from bouncing around from place to place like balls in a pinball machine. I was eager to settle for good. Although I was dismayed by my first views of this sere Chihuahuan Desert country, I was determined to make it my home. That has not been easy.

Both landscape and culture are foreign to me, so different from anything that I have ever called home that I have had to start from scratch to build a relationship. I thought that if I simply learned the plants and the animals, the names of the peaks and mesas and rocks, the biology of the desert, that familiarity would help me feel at home. Learning the facts and applying names to critters and places helped, but becoming an "expert," I realized, doesn't make a place home. I set out to look for cultural roots, learning the human stories of the desert—who lived here before us, who lives here now, and their relationship to this Chihuahuan Desert landscape. Knowing these stories helped me grow fond of the place, but there too, my relationship to the place remained an intellectual one. It still didn't feel like home. I was naive to think that I could move here and, by an effort of will, call this forbidding-to-me desert, home. I feel like I confidently jumped into a deep, swift river and then realized that I didn't know how to swim.

This terrifyingly hot and dry landscape, with its strange plants, animals, and human cultures, has taught me about myself. Home, I have learned, comes from within. I couldn't make the Chihuahuan Desert home by learning its facts and its stories, by intellectualizing the place. This difficult desert would not feel like home, I realized, until I was able to risk opening my heart to the place, until I could love it, embracing its painful contradictions, its harsh climate, its profoundly discomforting foreignness.

188

Coming south to live in this strange desert has taught me that I am not an explorer by nature. I am no conqueror of new worlds. I prefer to retrace familiar routes, coming to know them intimately, finding the new and novel in their details, observing how they change over time, not by charting new territory. I am a seeker of the wondrous in the familiar, the mundane, the overlooked everyday ordinary things. Moreover, I know now that I am most comfortable where I can blend in, where I can at least look like I belong.

That last is the most difficult. My pale skin and red-blond hair mark me a foreigner, and I am. I am by birth and inclination a *norteña*, a northerner. Until I moved to Las Cruces, I spent my entire life in the North, in a culture as different from this one as can be imagined. I was born and raised in the Midwest and settled in northern Wyoming as an adult. I grew up with pot roast and potatoes, quiet classical music, somber colors, the pared-down lines of Danish modern furniture, unadorned church services, and restrained emotions. Almost everyone looked like me, spoke the same language, held the same basic values, and could pronounce names like "Tweit" (which sounds like "Twight") on the first try. I fit there, in the land of snowy winters and white faces. It is hard to admit, but I prefer the comfort of familiarity to the challenge of the exotic. I'd like to belong.

If I need a reminder of my feelings of discomfort with this Chihuahuan Desert country, I need only look out my office window. There, among the hodge-podge landscaping of my suburb grow short, fat-trunked trees topped with tufts of green, fan-shaped leaves: palm trees. The sight of those palms is a continuing shock to me, an enduring reminder of how far I am from familiar northern landscapes and cultures. *189*

In my family history, however, there is a precedent for my journey south. In 1903, my great-grandfather, William Austin Cannon, moved south to study the neighboring Sonoran Desert. When I realized that he had made a similar journey before me, I wondered if the story of his years in that desert could help, perhaps by pointing the way for me to belong here. Unfortunately, I knew very little about him. As I read the sketchy information that I had on his life, I made a serendipitous discovery: An archive in Tucson, Arizona, possessed a collection of his letters dating from after his move south. Elated, I arranged to obtain copies. When the thick stack of letters, over a hundred pages of correspondence, arrived, I was so excited that I sat down to read them immediately.

The letters, written to Dr. Daniel T. MacDougal, director of the New York Botanical Garden, begin on September 15, 1903, three days after my great-grandfather disembarked from a Santa Fe Railroad passenger train in Tucson, Arizona. It was his first view of the Sonoran Desert, his first taste of the South. My great-grandfather, a native of Washington,

Michigan, and most recently assistant administrator of the New York Botanical Garden, had just taken the job as resident investigator at the brand-new Desert Botanical Laboratory, a center set up by the Carnegie Institute to study North America's deserts. The job, part chief scientist and part administrator, was a wonderful opportunity for an up-and-coming botanist like my great-grandfather. When he arrived in Tucson, he was just fifteen days short of his thirty-third birthday, bearing a new Ph.D. from Columbia University. He and his second wife, Jennie Vennerstrom, had a young son, Milner, my grandfather.

190

The deserts of North America were then new territory. No scientist had yet systematically studied the lives of the strange cacti, ocotillo, creosote bush, and other desert plants. No scientist had sorted out how these queer-looking life forms survived the intense heat and lengthy drought, much less how they interacted with each other and the desert environment. If my great-grandfather Cannon distinguished himself at his new post, his reputation as an independent scientist was assured. If not, he would likely spend his career as someone else's assistant. At his age, my great-grandfather wasn't likely to get another chance as promising as this new venture in the desert.

My great-grandfather Cannon wrote Dr. MacDougal nearly every day. (In that era before long-distance telephone service and electronic mail, the two scientists communicated by post, or, if something was especially urgent, by telegraph.) At first, my great-grandfather is wide-eyed, clearly wondering what he has gotten himself into, but no less game. "My dear Doctor MacDougal," he writes on September 15, 1903, three days after his arrival in Tucson, "The weather is supposed to

[be] very cool for this time of year, for which I am profoundly grateful. . . . I am willing to wait until another year before experiencing the hottest weather Tucson can put up. But," he assures his mentor and boss, "I think that I shall be able to do work here and that I shall like the climate. This certainly is a great country." Although he may be taken aback by the heat, the intense dryness, and the awesome emptiness of the desert—as well as the provincial character of Tucson in 1903— he doesn't let on. He is, after all, a competent Victorian man of science.

My great-grandfather is eager to settle in and get started on his research, to learn this strange desert, but that comes slowly. The laboratory building on Tumamoc Hill two miles west of downtown Tucson is still under construction. His days are filled with the minutiae of contractors and bills; the research must wait. In a letter to MacDougal detailing the progress on the lab building on September 27, my great-grandfather is optimistic—and frustrated: "We are going to have the nicest little laboratory going. The light is good and the building is convenient and there will be little disturbance from outsiders. . . . I am putting in my time attending to the innumerable small things which appear to come up as by magic, and in getting acquainted with the local conditions, and plants. The time is thus by no means lost." In another note that same day, enclosing a bill for the drinking water used during construction, my great-grandfather Cannon reports: "Mrs. Cannon and Milner came last evening. We are the guests of Mr. and Mrs. Hall, but shall be glad when the car [a railroad car bearing their furniture and belongings as well as the laboratory equipment] comes and we can get settled."

My great-grandfather's eagerness to begin learning this strange desert and establish his niche as a scientist continually collides with administrative chores. He writes to MacDougal a week later, on October 5:

> The mills of the gods grind very slowly indeed in this place but I hope that they grind exceeding fine. Progress however slight has been made since last I wrote you. . . . The electric light and telephone wires are at last up to the building. I induced the electric company to leave out the uppermost pole, the one next to the building, because it is so ugly as viewed against the Catalinas. As it is, the 2nd pole is sufficiently in evidence. I tried to get the electric people to ground the wires on the brow of the hill but the idea wasn't to their liking. That procession of poles straight up from the hospital is anything but beautiful; I suppose it is a necessary evil.

Later in the same letter, my great-grandfather Cannon mentions that he has been out exploring. The desert has already begun to draw him in: "I went to Gibbon's ranch (12 miles north east) on Saturday and examined and photographed some of the magnificent giant cacti which abound there. I saw some at least 50 feet high. That is a beautiful grove of them. . . . I am getting impatient to get to work. There are so many things to work at that it is too bad to waste much more time. We are thoroughly in love with this country already; I am hoping to take occasional excursions to see more of it."

Nearly two months later, the lab is finally set up, Professor and Mrs. Volney Spaulding, a visiting husband-and-wife research team, have arrived, and my great-grandfather has begun to settle into his own research. His letters to MacDougal sound less harried and anxious, and more excited and confident. November 23: "This is absolutely the finest place to work . . . that could possibly be found; I am more and more pleased with the prospects for research as the time goes on." Dec. 2: "I am having all kinds of fun with that Echinocactus [barrel cactus]. Prof. Spaulding thinks that I have a good lead. . . . There is much, if not everything, to be done yet on the morphology of it and ocatilla [sic], so that I am not out of employment."

Soon the Cannon family is getting settled too. In a letter to MacDougal on December 7, my great-grandfather reports with relief and a touch of humor that they have bought a lot and are living there in a tent while their house is under construction. "We enjoy the freedom from rent more than close association with the elements; but hope soon to have the one and avoid to a degree the other. . . . We will surely be glad when we are definitely and in a measure permanently located, and in our own house."

Everything about the desert piques my great-grandfather's wide-ranging curiosity. In early May of 1904 (the exact date of the handwritten letter is indecipherable), he writes MacDougal, "We have had a very cool, and dry, spring. The thermometer has not gone above 95°, and to that only once. Have had 1 inch of rain since September. . . . Had an encounter with a scorpion yesterday. Not worse than a bee sting." A few days later, May 17, comes his first desert thunderstorm, a real gully-washer. My great-grandfather is surprised and delighted at the effect of water on this brown desert. " [O]n Wednesday .75 in. of rain fell in less than half an hour. When I went down the mountain after it the water rushing down sounded like a cataract, the road to the hospital was covered and the flats this side of the Santa Cruz [River] were under water. More water came in those two days than was recorded at the University since September. As a result of this the plants on the hill are booming. The ocotillo began to come into leaf on Friday, the creosote bush is green again and the cacti are swollen and are brittle and easily broken."

Once his research is galloping along, my great-grandfather Cannon is settled in this strange desert landscape. Even the intense heat of his first summer doesn't slow the pace of his research—or dent his sense of humor. On June 13, he writes to MacDougal: "'Hits might hot' even in Arizona at 106°. I fear that Lloyd and Livingston [two visiting researchers] will feel the change considerably. Tucson is getting pretty well deserted now; everyone that can raise the money has gone to the 'Coast', and the rest will go in July. Even the most hardened liar among the natives hardly will defend this summer climate."

The desert took hold of my great-grandfather Cannon that first year and never let go. He built his career on desert ecology. Although he only spent fifteen years in the Sonoran Desert, two-thirds of my great-grandfather's fifty-plus scientific papers and books dealt with desert plants and ecology. (In 1918, he moved to the Carnegie Institute's Coastal Research Laboratory in Carmel, California and spent the rest of his life in California.) Over the years, my great-grandfather traveled to and studied deserts in other parts of the world, the Algerian Sahara, southwest Australia, and South Africa. His desert research yielded an illustrious career, including a listing in *American Men of Science* for forty years as one of the thousand top scientists in the nation.

I read my great-grandfather Cannon's letters with the hope that they would give me roots, show me how to belong in

this Chihuahuan Desert. I didn't find that. Most of his voluminous written conversation sticks to business. He rarely
mentions his feelings about the move or the difficulty of making a home in the strange new landscape. Nor was there any
reason for him to do so. My great-grandfather was, after all,
a Victorian man. He came to the Southwest and the desert,
not for a home, but for the opportunity it presented. For my
great-grandfather Cannon, the desert was an object of intellectual curiosity, a fertile source of scientific questions to answer, a place to make a reputation. He had no worries about
fitting in, about belonging.

Unlike my great-grandfather, I came south hoping to find
a home, to learn the place, to belong. To really know the
desert, I cannot follow in my great-grandfather's footsteps,
no matter how illustrious. I cannot maintain the same kind
of distance that served his science so well. To really know the
desert, I must get under its skin and learn the many stories of
all of its inhabitants—plants, animals (including humans), and
landscapes. To me, the desert is not just a fascinating landscape to study; it is a community to which I want to belong.
Reading my great-grandfather's letters told me that to really
know the desert, I must suspend my distance and dare to
enter into a personal relationship with this landscape. I must
risk my love.

❧

The morning is warming up by the time the twin lines of
pilgrims, including Denise, Dierdre, and me, reach the base
of Tortugas Mountain. The war captains stop the group there,
next to a cluster of porta-potties and a huge bonfire pile of
scrap wood and tires topped with creosote bush branches.
The leaders speak briefly, reminding us to climb carefully on

the rough trails up the mountain and asking for volunteers to carry up the tires for the luminarias that will be lit along the trails as the last of the pilgrims descend that night. Then they send us on our way. The orderly lines split into small groups as people head for the various trails leading to the top of the mountain.

Denise, Dierdre, and I decide to climb the "goat trail," a rough track that ascends straight up the mountainside. We join the stream of people slowly trudging up the rocky trail, stepping carefully because of the loose rock and the steep climb. We stop every so often to catch our breath and look at the view across the valley and West Mesa beyond. At one such stop, a barefoot woman passes us, leaning heavily on a walking stick with each slow step, her face drenched in sweat. We rest, then climb on.

Soon we reach the top of the mountain, crowded now with several thousand other pilgrims. Fragrant billows of smoke from the ceremonial fire of creosote bush drift across the mountaintop. We pick our way through the crowd to the open-air altar. Denise takes our veladoras and squeezes through the altar rail to place them on the pile of candles, retablos, and framed pictures of the Virgin of Guadalupe. Then we search for a sheltered spot out of the cold wind to rest and eat our snacks. Groups of people of all ages cluster around small fires, pulling lunches from coolers of food. The atmosphere is festive. People laugh, greet each other with *abrazos*—hugs—and share food.

Later, walking down the mountain in the warm afternoon sun, we are tired. We opt for the easiest route, the road that winds around the south side. Denise and Dierdre reminisce about old times. I walk quietly, overwhelmed by the day. As we come around the shoulder of the mountain, I notice the vegetation. The steep slopes around us are clothed in sparse clumps and mats of grass, now bleached to pale straw by winter. Here and there are shrubs, low, silvery-hairy mounds of range ratany, the occasional feathery olive-green canopy of creosote bush, tall, spiky clumps of yucca, and whiplike ocotillo stems reaching for the sky. And, studding the slope like giant pincushions, clumps of strawberry cactus, their hundreds of stems forming boulder-sized, spiny mounds. I interrupt Denise and Dierdre's conversation: "Look!" I exclaim, pointing excitedly to a nearby cactus mound several feet high and many feet in circumference. I tell them about the huge pink flowers that will bloom next spring, about how old these giant clumps of cacti surely are, and about the time that Richard and I first saw them bloom on a hot June evening. My words tumble over one another as I talk about the limestone that forms this unique mountain and about the enormous volcano that tilted those ancient layers skywards. I stop suddenly, embarrassed by my own enthusiasm. In the silence, Dierdre says, "I'm glad that you came. I've learned things that I didn't know I didn't know. Important things." Denise agrees, "I've lived here all my life, and I never knew these stories."

As we walk slowly down the mountain, our feet sore and our faces sunburnt, I understand. I've been looking for the wrong things. This is not Wyoming, the (relatively) green and fragrant landscape that touches my heart. It will never be. But I have come to love it all the same. I'll never be a native; I'll never blend in. I am an Anglo, a *norteña*, a foreigner—I can't change that. But I can belong. I can join the community of this Chihuahuan Desert country. The stories

197

that I have learned, the secrets and the magic of the desert, are my contribution, my membership card. I have something to give to this community of lives—its own stories. The forgotten stories, the stories that we didn't know we didn't know, the possibility, as Joy Harjo says, "of everything that we can't see."

Wallace Stegner once said that every place needs a poet, someone to sing its songs, to tell its stories. I think that Stegner meant *poet* in the sense of "loving, passionate, and knowledgeable advocate." I think that every place needs *many* poets, many voices, speaking for the rivers, the primroses and sphinx moths, the grizzlies, *las viejas*, the old ones—for all of the disappeared, the voiceless, the disenfranchised.

In searching out and telling the stories of this barren, wild, and worthless Chihuahuan Desert, I have come to love the place. In the doing, I have found a home. If I am forever a foreigner—no matter. Although I may never blend in here, I have earned my place. I belong.

urther Reading

Coming to the Chihuahuan Desert

Ann Hammond Zwinger's *The Mysterious Lands* (Plume, 1989) is a wonderful introduction to the four North American deserts, including the Chihuahuan. *Deserts* (Alfred A. Knopf, 1985), by James A. MacMahon includes a succinct explanation of what makes a desert a desert and what distinguishes the Chihuahuan from other deserts. Frederick Gehlbach's *Mountain Islands and Desert Seas: A Natural History of the U.S.–Mexican Borderlands* (Texas A&M University Press, 1981) looks at how human history has affected and continues to affect the ecosystems of *La Frontera*. Other views of how recent human history has changed the desert grasslands are found in *New Mexico Vegetation: Past, Present, and Future* (University of New Mexico Press, 1993) by William A. Dick-Peddie and *The Changing Mile* (University of Arizona Press, 1965) by James R. Hastings and Raymond M. Turner. *90 Years and 535 Miles: Vegetation Changes Along the Mexican Border* (University of New Mexico Press, 1987) by Robert R. Humphry is an especially poignant and graphic look. Technical articles such as J. L. Turner's "Vegetation of the Creosotebush Area of the Rio Grande Valley in New

Mexico," in *Ecological Monographs* (Vol. 2, 378–402, 1951) include fascinating historic accounts of the desert grasslands.

Spadefoot Toads and Storm Sewers

My essay on spadefoot toads and the changing land that they inhabit was inspired by Joseph Wood Krutch's classic on the Sonoran Desert, *The Desert Year* (Viking Press, 1963), and Gary Paul Nabhan's tales of desert plants in *Gathering the Desert* (University of Arizona Press, 1985). My information about spadefoot toads comes primarily from the scientific literature. A wonderful introduction is "Frogs and Toads in Deserts," in *Scientific American*, March 1994, by biologists Lon McClanahan, Rodolfo Ruibal, and Vaughn Shoemaker. Among the classic books on human history of the region are C.L. Sonnischen's *Tularosa* (University of New Mexico Press, reprint 1980), a book about the coming of cattle to this country, and Paul Horgan's mammoth *Great River: The Rio Grande in North American History* (Rinehart, 1954), a history of the river and its peoples. Michael Romero Taylor's edition of Bishop Henry Granjon's 1902 visit to the Mesilla Valley, *Along the Rio Grande* (University of New Mexico Press, 1986), is a charming look at the valley then.

The Disappeared Ones

My tale of grizzly bears in the Chihuahuan Desert region draws heavily from David A. Brown's *The Grizzly in the Southwest: Documentary of an Extinction* (University of Oklahoma Press, 1985). For more writings on grizzly bears, look for *The Great Bear* (Alaska Northwest Books, 1992), edited by John A. Murray. In writing the story of the Chihuahuan Desert Mogollon, I relied on the scientific literature. Interesting entries to that literature include *Dynamics of Southwest Pre-*

history (Smithsonian Institution Press, 1989), edited by Linda Cordell, and Polly Schaafsma's *Indian Rock Art of the Southwest* (University of New Mexico Press, 1980). One of the most fascinating places to learn about the culture of the *pochteca* at Casas Grandes is the Amerind Foundation Museum just off Interstate 10 at Dragoon in southeastern Arizona. Pat Beckett and Terry L. Corbett summarize new research on the Manso Indians in their monograph *The Manso Indians* (Coas Publishing, Monograph 9, 1992) and tell the story of Tortugas Pueblo in *Tortugas* (Coas Publishing, Monograph 8, 1990).

Weeds

201

For an understanding of the complicated problems of *La Frontera*, I recommend reading Earl Shorris's *Latinos: A Biography of the People* (W. W. Norton and Co., 1992) and Leon Metz' aptly named history, *Border* (Mangan Books, 1989). *Coyotes: A Journey through the Secret World of America's Illegal Aliens* (Random House, 1987), by Ted Conover, is a personal and horrifying look at migrant workers's journeys across the border. The American Friends Service Committee (Philadelphia, Pennsylvania) publishes a report of its Immigration Law Enforcement Monitoring Project every two years, a sobering account of abuse. For accounts of abuses, I drew on *Sealing the Borders: The Human Toll*, the 1992 report, and on conversations with Roberto Martinez, director of the Immigration Law Enforcement Monitoring Project in San Diego.

Sanctuary

A fascinating account of the tuberculosis epidemic and New Mexico's role as a "salubrious El Dorado" is in *Doctors of Medicine in New Mexico: A History of Health and Medical Practice, 1886–1986* (University of New Mexico Press, 1986), by Jake W. Spidle, Jr. In writing the history of Dripping Springs, I drew mainly from archival sources compiled by Katherine Durack for the Bureau of Land Management. "Jewel of the Organs," by Nena Singleton in *New Mexico* magazine (March 1990) is a popularly available sketch of Dripping Springs's history. William R. Seager's *Geology of the Organ Mountains and Southern San Andres Mountains, New Mexico* (New Mexico Bureau of Mines and Mineral Resources, Memoir 36, 1981) is the last word on the geology of the Organ Mountains.

202

Terminus

Marc Reisner's *Cadillac Desert: The American West and Its Disappearing Water* (Penguin, 1987) is required reading to understand water in the West. Gregory McNamee's *Gila: The Life and Death of an American River* (Orion Books, 1994) chronicles a Sonoran Desert river. *Once A River: Bird Life and Habitat Changes on the Middle Gila*, by Amadeo Rea (University of Arizona Press, 1983) is a poignant look at what "beneficial" use has done to one part of the same river. To understand the development of water law and water use in New Mexico, one must read Ira Clark's voluminous *Water in New Mexico: A History of Its Management and Use* (University of New Mexico Press, 1989). John Russell Bartlett's two-volume *Personal Narrative of Explorations and Incidents in Texas, New Mexico, California, Sonora, and Chihuahua* (D. Appleton & Co., 1856) is a fascinating look at the southwestern deserts 150 years ago. Much of the specific history of the Mimbres River comes from files in the Deming office of the New Mexico State Engineer. The groundwater geology comes from technical reports, including "Geology and

Underground Waters of Luna County, New Mexico," by N. H. Darton (U. S. Geological Survey, Bulletin 618, 1914). Water-use data comes from "Water Use by Categories in New Mexico Counties and River Basins," by Brian C. Wilson (New Mexico State Engineer Office, Tech. Rept. 47, 1992). For a look at the fissures of the Mimbres Basin, read "Ground-Water Overdraft and Land Subsidence," by William C. Haneberg (New Mexico Bureau of Mines and Mineral Resources, *Lite Geology*, Spring 1993).

Going South

My story of my great-grandfather's journey south comes from his letters, brought to my attention by Janice Bower's article, "William A. Cannon: The Sonoran Desert's First Resident Ecologist," (*Madroño*, Vol. 37, No. 1, 6–27, 1990). Pat Beckett and Terry L. Corbett's monograph *Tortugas* (Coas Publishing, Monograph 8, 1990) is one of the best sources on Tortugas and the Fiesta of *Nuestra Señora de Guadalupe*.

Source Credits

"Thoughts on a Dry Land," by Wallace Stegner, from *Where the Bluebird Sings to the Lemonade Springs* (New York: Random House, 1992).

"Unrefined" by Pat Mora is reprinted by permission from the publisher of *Chants* (Houston: Arte Público Press, University of Houston, 1985).

Terry Tempest Williams excerpt from *Writing Natural History: Dialogues with Authors,* edited by Edward Lueders. © 1989 by the University of Utah Press. Used by permission of the University of Utah Press.

Excerpts from *Secrets from the Center of the World,* by Joy Harjo and Stephen Strom. © 1989 by The Arizona Board of Regents. Printed by permission of the University of Arizona Press.

About the Author

Award-winning author and columnist Susan J. Tweit writes for *Audubon Magazine*, the *Denver Post*, and *Writers on the Range* syndicate. She is the author of seven books on the nature of the American West, including *Seasons on the Desert: A Naturalist's Notebook* and *City Foxes*, named an Outstanding Science Trade Book for Children for 1998.

A portion of the royalties from the sale of *Barren, Wild, and Worthless* will be donated to the New Mexico Nature Conservancy.